Kathy Van Horn, MEd, LP

realizing

[brain]

potential

A trauma-informed curriculum adapted with permission from the work of Bruce D. Perry and the ChildTrauma Academy.

Published by Lakeside
1350 Welsh Road, Suite 400, North Wales, PA 19454
(P) 215-654-9414 • www.lakesidelink.com

Information in this curriculum is adapted with permission from the Neurosequential Model of Therapeutics
(NMT) and the Neurosequential Model of Education (NME) developed by the ChildTrauma Academy. For more
information about the Neurosequential Model and the ChildTrauma Academy visit www.ChildTrauma.org

The excerpt in Chapter 17 is from *Waking the Tiger: Healing Trauma* by Peter A. Levine with Ann
Frederick, published by North Atlantic Books, copyright © 1997 by Peter A. Levine. Reprinted by
permission of the publisher.

Design: Ken Van Horn and John Ruffin
Photography: Kate Toussaint and iStockphoto
Editors: Shana Bushyhead Condill and Abigail Young

This will be an excellent resource for educators, and students will enjoy learning about the brain, stress, trauma, and resilience. Highly recommended.

BRUCE D. PERRY, M.D., PH.D.

The NeuroLogic® Curriculum represents an exciting and successful collaboration between Dr. Bruce Perry and the NeuroLogic® Initiative at Lakeside. The curriculum will help schools create trauma-informed classrooms that support brain-based learning and development while helping challenged children have breakthrough experiences in learning. Teachers, students, and parents will find the material to be accessible, interesting and novel, with suggestions for moving challenged children's minds out of the ruts they often find themselves in and revealing new opportunities for creative growth.

SANDRA L. BLOOM, M.D.

"Neurologic® provides an objective approach for students to connect the dots about their reactions and see that it's not always their "fault", they can blame it on their brain. From this vantage point exploring how to help myself is less, "I'm a bad person' and more, "I can practice activities that bring change". The Neurologic® curriculum offers a clear approach that is easily taught and makes so much sense.

KATHE DESANCTIS-MOYER, LPC, NCC, MA, BSN

The curriculum explains a lot of the things that have worked in my career working with kids who have experienced trauma. It helped me understand why certain things worked with these kids so I could be more intentional about it moving forward.

JAMES ROUTH, MA, LPC

I felt like it gave me more options that I didn't know about. . . . Students won't know what will help them unless it is put in front of them and they are able to experiment with the things that you have given them because they will have no idea unless they try it.

12TH-GRADE STUDENT,
LAKESIDE SCHOOL, NORTH WALES, PA

I feel as though this helps me get through a lot of unreasonable situations. . . . As my counselor spoke about the brain and how it functions, it gave me a better understanding of why and how those things in that class can help me in everyday life. It's a pretty good process. This has been helping me to maintain my composure pretty much. Now I feel as though I don't even have to result back to fighting and all of that. I feel as though I can just speak my piece and walk away.

11THGRADE STUDENT,
LAKESIDE SCHOOL, NORTH WALES, PA

Dedication

- To our students who inspire us all though their passion and perseverance as they work to overcome obstacles and achieve success.

- To Lakeside staff whose unwavering commitment, collective giftedness, and unconditional love change lives everyday.

- To Lakeside's facility dogs who keep us smiling *and regulated.*

About the Author

KATHY VAN HORN, MEd is a licensed psychologist, certified teacher, and certified school counselor. She has been working in the field of education for over 40 years and has spent the last 35 years as a teacher, counselor, supervisor, and administrator working for Lakeside. She currently is Executive Vice President of Lakeside and works part-time as a professor in Eastern University's graduate school counseling department.

Kathy has been trained by the ChildTrauma Academy in the Neurosequential Model of both Therapeutics and Education. She has used this training to help transform Lakeside schools into model trauma-informed programs. The NeuroLogic® Curriculum has been developed during this time in an effort to teach these very important concepts to Lakeside students. During the past five years, Kathy has been consulting and training school personnel both nationally and internationally through Lakeside's NeuroLogic® Initiative.

Lakeside and the NeuroLogic® Initiative

For nearly sixty years, Lakeside has been developing a comprehensive range of therapeutic educational services for students in and around the Philadelphia region. At the core of each program is the underlying belief that every student can be successful. With the right systems and interventions, we have seen this to be true with tens of thousands of students we have had the privilege to serve.

As our reputation for excellence has grown, many schools, organizations, and individuals have sought us out for our expertise, initiating the formation of our training division, Lakeside Global Institute. NeuroLogic® Initiative is a division of this Institute and focuses on practical trauma-informed training for schools, organizations, and individuals working with children. Through the NeuroLogic® Initiative, we have trained and coached professionals, across the country and around the world in understanding and applying practical brain-based, trauma-informed interventions to their work with students.

Not only does Lakeside help students experience success in school and life, we train others to do the same. If you would be interested in learning more about the NeuroLogic® Initiative, visit www.neurologicinitiative.com or contact us at training@lakesidelink.com.

Table of Contents

NeuroLogic® curriculum

Acknowledgments

This curriculum includes aspects of the work of many experts in the areas of education, trauma, neuroscience, psychiatry, and psychology, but the foundation and inspiration for the majority of these lessons is the work of Dr. Bruce D. Perry and the ChildTrauma Academy. Dr. Perry's work and the training provided by the ChildTrauma Academy on the Neurosequential Model of Therapeutics (NMT) and the Neurosequential Model of Education (NME) inspired the writing of this curriculum and provides hope and direction for those working with children who have been impacted by trauma or neglect.

Completing this curriculum has been a team effort. Thanks, Dr. Perry, for giving your time to review this curriculum and providing input, support, and direction. Dr. Sandra Bloom, thanks for your review, input and many helpful suggestions. Thanks, Diane Wagenhals, for sharing your vast knowledge and resources on the topic of trauma. Heidi Beatty, thanks for teaching these lessons over and over again to many groups of students with varying levels of interest and ability. You have researched ideas, supplied feedback and helped in refining this curriculum to work well for students. You have been a huge support throughout this process. Thanks, Joshua MacNeill, for your help in reviewing and supplying excellent ideas for activities and brain breaks. Your creative ideas, understanding of students, and expertise as a teacher have contributed significantly. Finally, thanks, Ken Van Horn, for your art direction as well as your constant support and encouragement.

Preface

Welcome to NeuroLogic®

This curriculum is a trauma-informed guide to empower students to explore the amazing learning and healing potential of their brains. This is intended to be used as a group curriculum for counselors or teachers working in schools, or other organizations. It can also be adapted for use with individual students. It is important that those teaching it are informed about, and sensitive to, the impacts of trauma. This curriculum does not, however, delve deeply into trauma-related therapeutic issues or the intricate details of the brain and neuroscience. It is based on sound information from the fields of neuroscience, psychology, and education, but written with the intention of being understandable, practical, and beneficial for all students.

It is important that students understand the impact that trauma and early childhood adverse experiences have on the developing brain. It is even more important they know what to do about it so there is hope and direction for healing and change. The word "trauma" will not be found in every lesson. This curriculum is meant to be used with all students, whether they have experienced trauma or not. We have found the use of the word "trauma" to be a trigger for some students and a turn-off for others. We have purposefully stayed away from using this term until later in the curriculum when a basic understanding of the brain and the brain's amazing potential to heal and change has been solidified. We encourage anyone teaching this curriculum to do the same.

Understanding the brain can help all students better recognize and manage emotions, control responses to stress, increase learning, and improve relationships. In adolescence, students' brains and bodies are being inundated with a range of hormones and a barrage of new emotions and sensations. This curriculum can help all students better understand themselves and their impact on others. It can empower students to take control of their learning and to better regulate their emotions and impulses.

These lessons are designed to encourage students to maximize their

Understanding the brain can help all students better recognize and manage emotions, control responses to stress, increase learning, and improve relationships.

potential. The information and activities included have the power to change the brain. The theme throughout these lessons is that change is possible. No matter what adversity a person has experienced in life, by understanding the brain more fully and applying this knowledge, he or she can bring about positive change, improved learning, emotional healing, and growth.

Introduction

Teaching These Lessons

This curriculum is written in terms of chapters rather than lessons. Each chapter contains information to be taught, activities to increase learning, and brain breaks to keep the students focused and prepared to learn. Each chapter is designed to take approximately 42 minutes. Depending on your students' ability level, attention span, and interest level, you may find that the time needed for lessons varies from class to class. Optional activities are provided throughout. You may use these in place of other activities or to expand a lesson over several class periods if you would like to take more time to focus on a particular topic.

The content and structure of these chapters repetitively demonstrate for students how the brain learns and changes. Learning requires not only giving information (firing neurons), but also building pathways so that information can be retrieved (wiring pathways). Neural pathways are wired through repetition. For this reason, it is important to allow students the time and opportunity to work through this information in a recursive manner. You will find many suggestions and opportunities for review and repetition of important concepts throughout the curriculum.

It is also important that information is presented in a variety of formats so it can enter the brain through different pathways. Having students respond through discussion, reflection, writing, movement, doodling, and various activities will help students recall and access the information learned. Each chapter offers suggestions for presenting the information, and choices for student responses.

Talk with students during the lessons about the strategies you are using and why you are using them. When you explain how a strategy or activity works based on what is known about the brain and learning, it becomes more powerful in shaping students' attitudes and learning. As you model brain-friendly approaches through your instruction, students will repetitively practice how to learn, and also how to make new, or strengthen existing, connections in their brains.

Biochemist, James Zull states that the most important factor in learning is the learner's existing neural network. He tells us, "We must let our students use the neuronal networks they already have. We cannot create new ones out of thin air or by putting them on a blackboard. And we cannot excise old ones. The only recourse we have is to begin with what the learner brings."[1]

For this reason, each chapter begins with a **"Making Connections"** section that draws on prior knowledge and prepares the brain to connect the new information to that knowledge.

This is followed up with a **"Preparing the Brain"** section that not only teaches the students an important regulation technique, but also helps calm the brain and prepares it to take in the new information.

The **"Instruction"** section of each chapter presents new information to be taught, along with suggested activities to help teach the new concepts. You will be able to pick and choose which information, what amount of information, and which activities are best for the students with whom you are working. Since the brain needs movement and activity to remain in an alert state and take in information, there are suggestions throughout each chapter for including movement. The brain learns best when information can be discussed and applied to real life, so each chapter also provides ample opportunities for discussion and application.

In order to put information into long-term memory, the brain needs time for reflection. For this reason, don't worry too much about daydreaming students. Daydreaming may be exactly what their brains need in order to learn. Some ways to allow time for reflection could be pausing for 20-30 seconds before moving on to a new topic, doing a brain break activity, giving students time to respond through writing or doodling, and using mindfulness or breathing activities. Towards the end of each chapter is a **"Reflection"** section. This section offers mindfulness exercises that allow students to learn this important regulation skill, as well as give their brains time to move information into long-term memory.

Lastly, each chapter ends with a time for reflection and application through journaling. The **"Journal"** section allows students time to creatively express their responses as they reflect on experiences and consider steps to take in light of what they have learned.

STUDENT WORKBOOKS

It is highly recommended that you use the student workbooks designed to go along with this curriculum. These workbooks include a summary of the key points of each lesson to remind students of all they have learned. There are focusing questions for students to answer throughout the lessons as well as a section for reflection to help students process and apply their learning. Lastly, a focus on gratitude will help students train their brains to shift to a calmer, more positive mindset.

ENSURING A SAFE ENVIRONMENT FOR LEARNING

The first lesson is focused on setting the groundwork for safety. It is important to set group rules and expectations for your classroom environment during the first class, to ensure students have a safe place for learning and processing information. As a group, brainstorm what a safe learning environment looks like physically, emotionally, and socially. Use this brainstorming session to set agreed-upon rules and expectations to ensure your classroom is a safe place for students to learn.

All students have their own unique background, outlook, skill set, personality, and previous experiences. Not all students will take in information or react to it in the same way. Some information and/or discussions may trigger a fight, flight, or freeze response for some students. Let students know that if the information or discussions at any time cause them to feel angry, anxious, unsafe, or threatened, they have options to keep themselves safe. Brainstorm the options for safety that are available for your students during the first class, and have students write a personal safety plan that they will keep with them throughout the course.

It is important that you, as the leader, take care of yourself so you can come to class as prepared and calm as possible. Your emotions and enthusiasm will be contagious. Recognize that, as the leader, your nonverbal communication will have as much, if not more, power as your verbal communication. Your relationships with students and reactions to students will set the stage for an inviting and safe environment conducive to learning. Even when dealing with behavior issues, it is important to deal with students in a calm, respectful, and caring manner.

PREPARING VISUALS AND ACTIVITIES

It is helpful to use a variety of methods of presentation to help students learn. Tangible objects students can see and touch will increase recall of the information taught. John Medina states, "We learn and remember best by pictures, not through written or spoken words. Vision trumps all other senses."[2]

Before the course begins, gather objects to put into a brain box that can be used to represent each topic. During each lesson, pull an object out of the box to signify the concept for that day. Students can pass around the objects to allow the information to enter their brains through not only the auditory pathway but also through the visual pathway and sense of touch. In future classes, each item used can be pulled out of the box to review information. The more senses you use while teaching the information, the more neural pathways you create allowing students to store and retrieve the information more efficiently. Here are some suggested items to put in your brain box:[3]

- Brain plasticity can be represented by play dough, silly putty, thinking putty, or different kinds of plastic items.
- Brainstem can be represented by a pulse oximeter, stethoscope, or thermometer.
- Midbrain can be represented by a plastic reptile, crayons, a small hand weight, or anything that represents fine motor or large motor movement.
- Limbic system can be represented by a heart, family picture, or anything that represents emotions or relationships.
- Cortex can be represented by a chess piece, crossword puzzle, calculator,

"We learn and remember best by pictures, not through written or spoken words. Vision trumps all other senses."[2]

JOHN MEDINA

book, reading glasses, or anything that represents higher level thinking, decision making, and problem-solving.

- Forming new neural connections can be represented by making trees and branches with pipe cleaners (See appendix A).

USING BRAIN BREAKS

Brain breaks are exactly what they sound like, a break for your brain. Your brain is constantly flowing in and out of direct attention as you are learning. Even if you are extremely interested in a topic, your brain will take an idea and begin to process it, while only paying peripheral attention to any new information coming in. Planning consistent brain breaks allows you to build that processing time into your class period for your students.

Brain breaks have the power to serve multiple purposes: they can help to wake students up, calm them down, or redirect their focus to make it easier to concentrate. Additionally, brain breaks can be individualized to address the brain region from which your students are operating. You may find that your students need a brain break as they come into the classroom, or that it is necessary later as they begin to lose focus.

Suggestions for brain breaks and brain-based educational activities are located throughout this curriculum. Familiarize yourself with these activities so that you are prepared and comfortable working them into each lesson as needed. Students are a lot more likely to buy in if the instructor leading the brain break is prepared and confident in leading it. Do not penalize students who do not participate in the brain breaks. They are still getting a brief break from learning and will hopefully participate eventually.

The need for brain breaks will be different for every group. You may find that your students need a brain break beyond the time suggested. Be creative and feel free to add your own calming and focusing brain breaks. An excellent resource with additional ideas for brain breaks that focus on each region of the brain is *101 Brain Breaks & Brain Based Educational Activities*[4].

Have fun as you implement these, and recognize that you will benefit from them as well. Even teachers need a quick break during class time to let their brains process what is going on. Don't be afraid to repeat activities that your students like, or modify the activities in a way that your students would be more receptive to.

BREATHING AND MINDFULNESS EXERCISES

You will find breathing and mindfulness exercises included in each of the lessons as a consistent form of a brain break. A breathing exercise is offered at the beginning to help students calm down and prepare their brains for learning. Our hearts and brains are intricately connected. A focus on breathing is a fantastic way to teach students to control their heart rates. Deep breathing biologically regulates the mind and the body. It improves the flow of oxygen to the brain, improving the brain's ability to process information.

Each lesson ends with a mindfulness exercise, prior to a journaling activity. These exercises vary from opportunities for students to process the specific information shared, to opportunities for students to be more mindful of the things going on within their bodies and the impact certain stimuli might have on them. These exercises are presented towards the end of each chapter to help prepare the students to look inward for a more meaningful time while journaling. Mindfulness exercises can promote the integration of the brainstem, limbic system, and cortex by creating new neural pathways. They can reduce stress and improve attention and memory.[5]

Please note that these activities may seem awkward at first for many of your students. In fact, if you have not done them before, they will likely feel awkward to you. It is important to persevere through any awkwardness you and your students may be feeling. These exercises are important skills your students will need for regulation, and they can have a positive domino effect in your classes. One by one, students will begin to buy in when they see other students participating and recognize the positive impact the activities seem to have on their classmates.

You may find that some students choose not to participate in these exercises. That is okay; they are still being exposed to them and, if nothing else, are experiencing a couple of minutes of quiet. They are still observing and possibly learning several activities that could benefit them. They may later attempt these activities in a place where they feel safe. Do not force your students to participate, as that can have an adverse impact. Make sure, however, that you include rules and expectations for your class that include being quiet and respectful during all exercises so as not to disrupt those who are choosing to participate.

Because teenagers are so focused on technology, it may be helpful to work technology and/or technology metaphors into your teaching about breathing and mindfulness. You can talk about these breaks as times to go offline to reset or reboot their systems. Also, there are a lot of great mindfulness and breathing "apps" available that students can use to help them focus on breathing and mindfulness. If you decide to use "apps," make sure to also teach the skills without the "apps," and support students in finding ways to be mindful while taking breaks from technology.

Finally, as you discover what works best with your students, you may find that they gravitate towards specific breathing and mindfulness exercises. You can repeat these at any time and use them throughout the lessons. The only difference between these activities and a typical brain break is that they are tied to a particular place and purpose in the lesson. All of these exercises are fantastic ways to give the brain a break to process and prepare for the next phase of learning.

Deep breathing biologically regulates the mind and the body. It improves the flow of oxygen to the brain, improving the brain's ability to process information.

Creating Safety

1

Creating Safety

Objectives & Materials

STUDENTS WILL BE ABLE TO:
- Collaboratively determine rules and expectations for safety
- Recognize the connection between the heart and the brain
- Discuss four dimensions of safety
- Write a personal safety plan
- Complete a pre-course survey

MATERIALS:
- Flip chart paper and markers for listing ground rules
- Pre-course survey
- Workbooks or safety plan handout
- Pulse oximeters if available
- Thumb ball

SETTING TONE, GROUND RULES, AND EXPECTATIONS

During the first class, make sure to set the tone and structure for safety and learning. (See pages 12-13.) Let students know that you are committed to treating them with respect and expect them to do the same for you and for each other. Be sure to model this behavior throughout the course, especially in how you respond to students involved in negative behaviors.

Be aware that your emotions are contagious and what you bring into the class will impact your students. Your ability to stay calm and caring while maintaining classroom rules and boundaries will have a significant impact on your students. A leader that ensures a safe environment for all students will increase positive emotions, and positive emotions will increase learning.

It is best to work collaboratively with class members to formulate rules and expectations for safety. This lesson will guide you through this process. Before starting, you may want to find out what students think about classroom rules and safety in general.

Making Connections

BUILDING COMMUNITY

Before starting the lesson today, it's important to spend some time allowing students to get to know each other and feel comfortable together. Use a thumb ball with questions on it (or numbers on it and questions on the board). You can buy thumb balls or make them. (See resource section in Appendix C.) Have students throw the ball to each other and share their name and non-threatening information about themselves in response to the question where their thumb lands on the ball. Depending on the comfort level of your group, you may find it helpful to start with some type of community building each session.

Preparing the Brain

HEART RATE

Introduce the Heart Rate Activity with the following background information for the students:

Your brain and heart are connected. Your heart rate is an indication of what is going on in the lower levels of your brain. In this course, you will track your heart rate before and after activities in each session. This can help you understand what is going on in your body and brain. Some activities will be calming, bringing your heart rate down; some may have no significant impact; and others will be alerting, bringing your heart rate up. Understanding the impact of these experiences on your heart rate can empower you with new ideas and choices for self-regulation and stress reduction. Check your heart rate and record it in the heart rate chart in the front of your workbook. There are sections to record your heart rate before and after an activity. You can record it more often if you would like. The comments section of the chart is for you to record what you were feeling, doing, or experiencing that may have caused a change in your heart rate.

ACTIVITY

Have students take their pulse and document it on a heart rate chart. Students can use pulse oximeters if available, take their pulse by hand, or use a heart rate "app." Inform students of the importance of the brain being calm in order to best take in new information. Have students experiment with breathing rapidly and then taking slow deep breaths to see what impact this may have on their heart rate. Make sure to end this activity with students taking slow deep breaths to prepare the brain for learning.

PULSE OXIMETER

A pulse oximeter is a non-invasive device that clips onto your finger and reads your heart rate as well as the percent of oxygen that's in your blood. The oxygen level reading is designated under SPO2; the other number will be your heart rate (designated as HR, PR, or BPM). In this course, we will be focusing mostly on heart rate. Excessive movement may result in the pulse oximeter providing either an inaccurate heart rate reading or no reading at all. Try to remain relatively still while the pulse oximeter is taking its reading. Also, nail polish may keep the oximeter from reading your pulse. If this is the case, turn your finger sideways.

Instruction

Complete the following exercise with your students:

> What do you think people need in order to be comfortable enough to share their thoughts and feelings? What do you need? Write down 3–5 rules or expectations that you think would be important for us to follow during our time together. We will be going over these and combining our lists in a little while. Feel free to add to your list as you think of things.

In order to learn and try new things, it is important that you feel safe. There are two aspects of safety that we need to address today. First, we will address group safety by brainstorming and setting expectations and rules for the time we are together. After this, we will take some time for you each to write a personal safety plan. It is possible as we go through this course that some of you may at times feel uncomfortable, overwhelmed, anxious, or fearful. A personal safety plan will prepare you with both the permission and power to keep yourself safe.

Dr. Sandra Bloom in her book, *Creating Sanctuary*, talks about the need for physical, psychological, social, and moral safety.[6] It may help to refer to these while students brainstorm.

Creating a positive learning community

- **Physical Safety** – Knowing that your body will not be hurt by others or by yourself.
- **Emotional Safety** – Being safe with your feelings and knowing how to take care of yourself when your feelings become uncomfortable.
- **Social Safety** – Feeling safe and cared about within a group.
- **Moral Safety** – Knowing right from wrong and trusting the people around you know right from wrong.

SAFETY ACTIVITY

After discussing the importance of creating a safe environment and Dr. Sandra Bloom's four categories of safety, use this activity to discover what the students find most important for their safety. Post the four categories of safety in the four corners of the room, ask students to take a moment to consider which they find to be most important, and then go stand in the corner that represents their decision. Once everyone has picked a corner, encourage the class to look around for a moment to recognize that everyone defines safety a little differently. (If you find that the majority of students went to the same corner, or two corners, use it as a way of helping the students to see how similar they are to one another.)

While they are still standing, go around the room and ask each student, if they are willing, to share why they chose the corner they did. If any corner is not represented, ask the class to consider why no one went there. Ask students if this was an easy decision, or if they are all important to them and they struggled to make their choice. Do they think their decision would always be the same? Do their priorities of safety change throughout the course of the day? Week? Year? After the discussion, invite your students to head back to their seats.

Based on their original lists and what they have just learned from each other, work together as a class to create a list of classroom expectations for the group. You can write these up on the board or allow a couple of your students to work as scribes, writing on the board. Make sure each student has the opportunity to have a say. If they are struggling to get started, or missing something that you think is important, make suggestions to help guide them. Remember to ask students what they expect from you as the leader, and add to the list what you expect from them. At the end of this discussion, you and the class members should agree on a list of rules to follow while together in this class.

Try to keep the rules in a positive format, as close to their language as possible, and appropriate to your environment. Make sure the rules are clear and easily understood. The following are some examples of rules and expectations to consider:
- Respect the opinions and experiences of others.
- Listen. Allow others to talk without interruption.
- Keep your hands to yourself.
- Respect personal space and property.
- Be kind in words, tone, and facial expressions.
- Keep an open mind. Some activities may seem silly to you. Try them anyway.
- New experiences may cause anxiety. Allow others to pass when needed.
- Allow yourself and others the opportunity to try things and repeat activities as many times as needed to learn.

PERSONAL SAFETY PLANS

Dr. Sandra Bloom in *Creating Sanctuary* and Diane Wagenhals in *Enhancing Trauma Awareness* both talk about the importance of creating personal safety plans. Because some of the material in this curriculum has the potential to trigger a student's past traumatic experiences or create high levels of stress, it is important that each student has the opportunity to create a personal safety plan. They may want to write different safety plans for different situations, such as one for home, one for class, one for activities with friends, etc.

According to Diane Wagenhals, a safety plan is "a predetermined list of ways a person can mentally or physically ensure they stay safe, especially if a topic, activity or environment is perceived as potentially dangerous or threatening." Wagenhals writes about both internal and external safety plans.[7] It is helpful to discuss with students what a safety plan is, when it is needed, and why it is beneficial.

Give students examples of both internal and external options that might be included in a safety plan for school. Some possible options are listed below. Choose the ones that are possible and that will not be disruptive to your classroom.

INTERNAL SAFETY PLAN OPTIONS
* Picture a safe and peaceful place where you feel comfortable.
* Mentally acknowledge your power to maintain your safety.
* Focus on your breathing, taking slow and deep breaths.
* Zone out for a few minutes.
* Repeat a positive statement to yourself. "I am safe." "I am not in danger."
* Relax your body.
* Be mindful of the present and focus on a specific sound, sight, smell, or sensation.

EXTERNAL SAFETY PLAN OPTIONS
* Sit in a part of the room where you feel safest.
* Sit next to someone with whom you feel safe.
* Pass on an activity or discussion question.
* Remove yourself from the group.
* Ask to get a drink of water or go to the bathroom.
* Put your head down and/or close your eyes for a few minutes.
* Distract yourself by doodling, journaling, or tapping the back of your hand.
* Use a picture or tangible object to distract yourself.
* Tell someone you trust that you are feeling unsafe.

There is no right or wrong way to write a safety plan. All students need to think about their own triggers and what will help them feel safe. One way to help students think this through is to ask them to write down particular emotions with which they have problems. Once the emotions are identified, have them write down the situations that are most likely to stir up those emotions. With these situations in mind, they can more easily write a safety plan focused on ways to better manage each situation.

Give students time to write their safety plan for this class on an index card or in their workbooks. Encourage them to choose from the list of suggestions or to create their own items. If time allows, have them write safety plans for other situations. If time does not allow, encourage them to continue this activity in their workbooks after class. The safety plan for this class should be kept in a place that is accessible to them during every class.

PRE-COURSE SURVEY
Before moving on with the following lessons, let the students know that you will have them complete a survey to find out what their current understanding and perspective is about their brains and what they are currently doing to regulate their emotions and behaviors. This same survey will then be used at the end of the course to see what, if anything, has changed.

"Mindfulness is noticing your thoughts, feelings, and physical sensations in the present moment without judgment in as many moments of your life as possible."[8]

GINA BIEGEL

Explain the importance of starting with what students already know, think, and do so the brain can make connections with already existing neural networks. Let them know that this will be an important part of every lesson. An analogy you can use is that of a clothes closet or dresser. If new clothes are put away in categories based on what is already there (e.g. shirts in top drawer, pants in bottom drawer, jackets in closet), it is much easier to find a specific item when you want it. If everything is thrown in a pile on the floor, it takes a lot longer to find what you want and some things can easily get lost. Let the students know that you will always attempt to start a lesson with a review of something they already know or think so that they can connect the new information and know in which drawer or part of the closet in their brain to put it.

Have students take the Pre-Course Survey. Make sure students know there are no right or wrong answers.

Reflection   SAFE PLACE
Introduce the mindfulness exercise for the students:

> We will be practicing mindfulness exercises towards the end of each class to give your brains a chance to reflect and process what has been taught. Mindfulness can improve your attention, focus, memory, emotional regulation, and learning. Basically, in mindfulness exercises, you take some time to focus on a particular thing. It could be something tangible outside your body, it could be a thought, or it could be a feeling or sensation.
>
> There is no right or wrong way to do mindfulness. You may find your thoughts drifting throughout these exercises to other things grabbing for your attention. This is natural. As thoughts enter your mind, acknowledge them and then move on, refocusing back to the topic of the mindfulness exercise. Attention is like a muscle. As you participate in mindfulness exercises throughout these lessons, you will find that your ability to focus your attention slowly expands. Today we will be focusing on what you picture when you think about a safe place for you.
>
> Block out distractions for a couple of minutes by closing your eyes, putting your head down or focusing on a spot on your desk or a wall. (Instructors, students who have experienced trauma may not feel comfortable closing their eyes so make sure to always give options.)
>
> Imagine a place where you can feel safe and calm. It can be anywhere you have ever been or a place you want to go. If you can't think of a place like this, imagine a place that you have seen on TV, or a place that you make up in your mind. Picture yourself in this place. Add as much detail as possible using all of your senses. What is around you? What do you see? What do you hear? What do you smell? What do you feel?

Are you sitting, standing, laying down, or walking? Is there anyone there with you? Continue to imagine this in as much detail as possible.

Journal

After a few minutes, encourage students to share about their safe place through writing, drawing or talking in pairs. Make sure each student has a journal and have art supplies available. Let students know journaling is their time to reflect and apply information learned in whatever way works for them. They can use words, colors, drawing or doodling.

Impact of Perspective

2

Impact of Perspective

Objectives
& Materials

STUDENTS WILL BE ABLE TO:
* Consider facts about the brain
* Understand the impact that perspective has on success
* Examine their own perspective in relationship to growth and change
* Reflect on the idea of brain plasticity
* Participate in a breathing exercise

MATERIALS:
* Student workbooks or survey

Making
Connections

ACTIVITY: BRAIN FACTS

Let students know the purpose of this activity is to get them thinking about what they currently know about the brain, so they will have something to connect new information to. (Remind students of the closet analogy from chapter one.)

On the board or on several pieces of flip-chart paper, have students write anything they know or have heard about the brain. Emphasize that there are no wrong answers. This activity will help you, the teacher, know what students think about the brain and what things they have learned about the brain in the past.

Once the answers are on the board, give the students a few seconds to review what their classmates wrote. Then, facilitate a discussion regarding what stood out to them. If the class does not arrive there by itself, you can add in how complex the brain is, and how vulnerable it is to being impacted by the world. Have some interesting brain facts available to share with students. Some ideas are listed below.

Brain Facts: This list is adapted from the website coolkidsfacts.com[9]
* Your brain recognizes your touch so you can't tickle yourself.

- The adult brain weighs about 3 pounds and is made up of primarily water and fat.
- Even though your brain is just 2% of your body weight, it uses 20% of all the energy from your blood and oxygen.
- Your brain is like a switchboard for your whole body. Everything that happens in your body affects your brain and your brain affects every part of your body.
- Music helps the two sides of your brain communicate.
- Dreaming involves more brain activity than anything you do while awake.
- Stress alters brain cells and functions, often making them too sensitive or breaking connections so that communication between the brain and its parts doesn't work properly.
- At birth, the vast majority of 86 billion neurons used for the remainder of life are present.
- It would take you over 3,000 years to count the 86 billion neurons in your brain.
- Your brain produces enough energy to power a light bulb.
- Sleep helps your brain store all your memories from the day. If you don't sleep, you could have trouble creating new memories.
- When you laugh, your brain is working overtime. Five areas of your brain need to work together for you to laugh.

Explain that there is lots of great information students will learn about the brain, all of which will be practical and helpful in empowering them to increase learning, understand themselves and others, manage intense emotions, deal with adversity, and overcome difficulties. Let them know that in order to change and grow, various parts of the brain need to be activated. This involves not only hearing new information but also seeing, touching, moving, and experiencing the information through activities such as discussions and journaling. For this reason, we will be doing lots of activities throughout this course.

Preparing the Brain

It is important to start with an exercise you feel will be most comfortable for your students. Square breathing is an easy breathing exercise to start with for most students.

As you teach a breathing exercise, encourage participation but do not penalize those students who do not participate. Maintain parameters for safety by reminding nonparticipating students of the need to respect those who do participate. Encourage all students to try the exercise by letting them know this is something that will help them. If some are not comfortable doing the exercise in front of others, encourage them to try it later on their own. Even students who do not participate will most likely regulate breathing as you model the exercise.

Don't worry if you meet with resistance. As you stick with these exercises, students will become more receptive. Start with doing the exercise for one minute. You will be able to increase the time for these exercises throughout the course as your students become more comfortable.

SQUARE BREATHING

Introduce the breathing activity:

> Today we are going to experiment further to see what can affect your pulse. Breathing can impact your heart rate and therefore your brain. We all breathe instinctively in order to stay alive. Focusing on breathing may seem silly or odd, yet breathing is a very powerful tool that can help you control your thoughts, feelings, behavior, and physiology. Slowing down your breathing helps slow down your heart rate. Slow, deep breathing increases the amount of oxygen that goes to your muscles, releasing tension. Focusing on breathing can slow down your thoughts and lower your anxiety level.
>
> As you attempt to focus on your breathing, recognize that it may take some practice. It may actually raise your heart rate as it is a new experience that can make you self-conscious or anxious. Remember that you are in control of this process. You can stop whenever you want. You can choose to close your eyes or keep them open, focusing on a point on the wall or floor. It is important to practice deep breathing in a place where you feel relatively safe and comfortable. You may feel silly or uncomfortable the first few times, but keep at it. With practice you will find that you are able to use this skill easily in many different situations. Practicing these activities on your own in a safe, quiet place outside of school will increase your comfort level with them.
>
> For today's breathing exercise we are going to do a very simple breathing exercise called square breathing. Using a visual with breathing helps to add rhythm and pattern. For square breathing you breathe in for a count of four, hold for a count of four, breathe out for a count of four, hold for a count of four, and then repeat. If you would like to add hand movements, you can trace a square in the air with one hand or trace a square on a desk or piece of paper. Check your heart rate and record it in the heart rate chart in the front of your workbook before and after the exercise.
>
> -Adapted from *Doodles, Dances and Ditties*[10]

> "He who breathes deepest lives most."[11]
>
> **ELIZABETH BARRETT BROWNING**

Instruction

SURVEY

The purpose of this survey is to get students thinking and talking about what they currently believe about their brains. Assure them there is no right or wrong answers, but that they should be prepared to talk about why they think what they think. Have the students fill out an individual survey. This will give them a chance to think through their answers before movement is required. Having students stand and move towards their answers will then help them see and consider what others think and will help them to better remember the discussion.

Read the questions out loud, one pair at a time, having students move to one side of the room or the other depending on what they chose. Always keep the *ones* on the same side and the *twos* on the opposite side. Once students have chosen a side to stand, have them discuss with those around them why they chose that statement. Keep this moving at a pace that feels right to you depending on the amount of discussion and comfort level of your students. If you find a few students are going to one side consistently and it is feeling awkward, speed it up by skipping some of the statements.

Have students circle one of the statements in each pair that they believe best reflects the way they think.

1. If I am not good at something, I probably never will be.
2. If I stick with something, I can get better at it.

1. If my first plan fails, I give up.
2. If my first plan fails, I can figure out another way to do it.

1. Making mistakes is embarrassing and a reason to stop trying.
2. Making mistakes is a chance to learn how to do it better next time.

1. My beliefs about people and the world are accurate and do not change much.
2. My beliefs about people and the world are flexible, and change with experiences.

1. You can only get straight As if you are naturally smart.
2. Anyone can get straight As if they work hard enough.

1. If you are impulsive, you will always be that way.
2. You can change how impulsive you are.

Afterwards, explain that the number 1 statements represent a perspective that limits growth. The number 2 statements represent the opposite perspective, one that leads towards growth. These two perspectives are what we will be learning about today.

CHANGING THE BRAIN

Our brains are loaded with billions of brain cells, but in order to work these cells must be connected to each other. The brain is a constant chemical factory that is being wired throughout childhood and adolescence. In addition, our brain's growth is dependent on how it is used. The good news is that the brain has plasticity, meaning that the brain has an amazing capacity to change. However, some parts of the brain are easier to change than others. In order to change a part of the brain, it has to be activated, which means that at times we need to "turn on" certain parts of our brains. We can do this by certain activities, and throughout this course we will be exploring how different activities can target a specific part of the brain. Before learning about how to change the brain, we first will examine our perspective

"Failure is a part of life. It's a part of building character and growing. Without failure, who would you be? I wouldn't be here if I hadn't fallen thousands of times, made mistakes.... If something's going on in your life and you're struggling, embrace it, because you're growing."[12]

NICK FOLES, SUPER BOWL LII MVP

regarding growth and change, because this perspective will impact our success. The following activity can help to introduce this concept to the class.

ACTIVITY

Give each student a supply of pipe cleaners. Have two sets of written instructions but don't let the students know that they are different. Hand out one set to the right side of the room and the other set to the left side. Tell students that once instructions are handed out, there will be no talking. Tell them to read the instructions to themselves and to look up when done, so you know when to start the timer. You can change the amount of time given for this activity or the height of tower you are going for, based on the needs and abilities of your students. Make your best estimation of the time it will take, and increase the length if needed.

One set of instructions should read:

You have three minutes to build a tower as high as possible with these supplies. The highest tower anyone has been able to build in three minutes is a tower three pipe cleaners high. This was accomplished by a group of graduate students in an engineering department. There is only one rule: whatever you do, don't let the tower fall as you are building it. If you do, you have to take it apart and start completely over. Good luck, let's see how you do.

The other set of instructions should read:

You have three minutes to build a tower as high as possible with these supplies. The highest tower any students have been able to build in three minutes so far is a tower six pipe cleaners high. This was accomplished by a group of students much younger than you. I'm sure many of you will beat this. Good luck, I know you will do well.

After three minutes, compare how the different sides of the room did. Hopefully the groups with the second set of instructions will have more significantly higher towers than the other side of the room. You may need to apologize to the side of the room with the first set of instructions, if they are discouraged. Share and discuss the difference in instructions. In the first instructions, mistakes are discouraged and low limits are set mentally, based on past experience. Students might be motivated in spite of the low expectations set, but the fear of mistakes can keep them from taking chances and trying out new ideas. In the second set of instructions, students are encouraged to keep working no matter how many times the tower falls and encouraged to believe that building a very high tower is possible. Discuss with students their feelings during this activity and how it might apply to other things in life.

30

▶ INSTRUCTORS NOTE: This is not a perfect activity. It may not work all the time, but it often works. If there is not a significant difference between towers, be prepared to still make your points. You can applaud students for not letting you fool them. Ask students why they think the limiting instructions didn't hinder them. Students may already have a strong positive perspective, or maybe they were inspired by seeing how the other side of the room was doing. If students with the second set of instructions did not do well, you can ask what hindered them and discuss the things in life that can hinder us all from doing well. Maybe students stopped trying because of comparing themselves to others, they didn't care about the activity, or they didn't want to look foolish or incapable.

IMPACT OF PERSPECTIVE

Psychologist and researcher Carol Dweck found one important difference between people who were more successful and those who were not. She calls this difference "mindset." She found that unsuccessful people had a mindset that was "fixed." They believed you were either born smart or talented or not. Successful people, on the other hand, believed in a growth mindset. They understood that you can get smarter by working on it and that talent and skills get better with practice.[14]

Dweck and colleagues did a study with students. The researchers taught one group of students how intelligence can change while the other group did not receive this information. Both groups were then taught identical information on study skills. The group that learned about how intelligence can change reversed their previously declining achievement scores and outscored the other group, whose scores continued to decline. Study skills training alone was not enough to improve scores. When students understood that the brain could change and they could take control of their learning, achievement increased.[15]

DISCUSSION
* Why do you think these two groups of students had different levels of success?
* Have you ever seen something like this be true for you?
* Can anyone think of a time when your perspective helped you achieve or was a part of your lack of achievement?
* What do you think it takes to have, or keep, a perspective that leads towards growth?

The brain is like a muscle. You can continue to grow and change any part of your brain throughout life. Change comes as a result of repetition, in the same way repetitive weight lifting will build your muscles. Repetitive activation of any area of your brain will change that part of the brain. When a part of your brain is activated over and over, it changes. To learn a new skill, you must practice it over and over again. Making mistakes is a natural part of learning. Mistakes allow you to recognize what doesn't work so that you can try a new or different solution.

"For thirty years, my research has shown that the view you adopt for yourself profoundly affects the way you lead your life. It can determine whether you become the person you want to be and whether you accomplish the things you value."[13]

CAROL S. DWECK

ACTIVITY

Review what you checked off on the survey. Number *ones* indicate a perspective that limits growth. Number *twos* indicate a perspective that leads towards growth. Which perspective do most of your checks fall under? Feel free to make changes to your survey if there is anything you want to change, based on the information you just learned.

Reflection

DISCUSSION

- Do you currently have more of a growth-limiting or growth-producing perspective?
- Do you have a different perspective at different times or for different areas of your life?
- Do you believe you can get better at the things you struggle with? Why or why not?

"The passion for stretching yourself and sticking to it, even (or especially) when it's not going well, is the hallmark of the growth mindset. This is the mindset that allows people to thrive during some of the most challenging times in their lives."[21]

CAROL S. DWECK

MINDFUL BREATHING

Introduce the mindfulness exercise:

In a few minutes you will have time to reflect and journal about what you have learned. In order to give your brain time to reflect and put this information into long-term memory, we will first do a mindfulness exercise that focuses on breathing. Your breath can be used as an anchor to keep you in touch with the here and now. Record your heart rate before we begin.

Find a comfortable sitting position. Close your eyes if you are comfortable, or focus on a point on your desk, floor, or wall. Take one minute of absolute silence and pay attention to your breathing. Notice as it moves through your body. Pay attention to where you feel it the most. Don't try to change it, just notice it. Where is the air coming into your body? Is it through your nose or mouth? Where does it go next? Can you feel the temperature of the air you breathe? Does the temperature change as it enters your body? What parts of your body move as the air comes in? What moves as the air goes out? Continue to breathe, just noticing what is happening and how it feels.

After one minute of silence, have students return their focus to you. Ask students to record their heart rate and then share their experiences.

- What was this experience like for you?
- What did you notice about your breathing?
- What did you feel? (This could include physical sensations or emotions.)
- Did your heart rate change after the exercise? If so, how?

Journal

Make sure each student has a journal and have art supplies available. Let students know journaling is their time to reflect and apply information learned in whatever way works for them. They can use words, colors, drawing or doodling.

3 Understanding Brain Plasticity

Understanding Brain Plasticity

Objectives & Materials

STUDENTS WILL BE ABLE TO:
- Reflect on varying degrees of brain plasticity
- Discuss examples of brain plasticity
- Contemplate personal impact of brain plasticity
- Practice a breathing exercise
- Practice a mindfulness exercise

MATERIALS:
- Different plastic objects
- Thinking putty or play dough
- Origami or airplane folding activity
- Small item to toss in the air or bounce

Making Connections

Compare two plastic objects, one that is very moldable and one that is less easy to change. This could be a plastic bag and a plastic trash can, a piece of plastic wrap and a firm plastic cup, etc. It doesn't really matter. The point is that plastic comes in all shapes and sizes and some types of plastic are more easily changed than others. Demonstrate for your students the difference and talk about how all plastic is changeable but not all can be changed easily. For some things it may take extreme heat to melt it, or something very sharp to cut into it. For other types of plastic, you can change the shape and size using your hand. This is what brain plasticity is like. All parts of the brain can change, but some are very hard to change compared to others. This lesson will be about brain plasticity.

Give each student a container of thinking putty, play dough, or some other moldable substance. Tell them throughout the lesson they should use the putty to remind themselves of their brain's ability to change and learn. If using thinking putty, they can note how the putty changes color as they handle it, and that even when not handling it, the shape can change. Make a perfect ball at some point during the lesson and let it sit without touching it. It will flatten out if given enough time.

Another idea for presenting plasticity and how the brain changes and makes new connections is with pipe cleaners. This analogy is presented in Appendix A.

Preparing the Brain

BELLY BREATHING

This activity is adapted from an exercise in *The Mindfulness Toolbox* by Donald Altman.[17] Introduce the breathing exercise:

> In the last lesson, you practiced square breathing and a mindful breathing exercise. Today, you will look a little more closely at how you breathe. Before you begin, take your pulse and write it in your chart. Now sit up straight in your chair and breathe normally. Keep breathing, but place one hand over your chest and one over your belly. Which hand is moving more? Is the air you are breathing traveling down to your belly, or is it stopping in your chest? Now reach your hands as far behind your back as you can without straining and keep breathing. Do you feel any difference in where the air you are breathing is going? Hold your arms back for 60 seconds and keep breathing. Put your hands back where they are comfortable, and when you are ready, take your pulse.
>
> When we are born we are all belly breathers. When you watch a baby breathe, you will see their belly going up and down. This is the ideal breathing method to get your body and brain what it needs. Belly breathing significantly increases the oxygen that is getting to your brain. Belly breathing promotes calmness and relaxation, where chest breathing can cause stress and anxiety. If you found yourself breathing more from your chest than your belly, you can change back to being a belly breather.
>
> In our last time together we talked about perspective, and the fact that you can change your perspective. Today we are talking about brain plasticity, which is the idea that you can actually change your brain for the better. By repeatedly focusing on your breathing and directing air into your belly, you are actually re-training your brain to breathe properly. If you find it difficult to breathe into your belly just by thinking about it, keep your hand on your belly to make sure it moves. Or you can reach your hands behind your back or behind your head to open up your ribcage, forcing the air to come down to your belly. As we do more breathing exercises in the coming classes, focus on breathing into your belly and see if it makes a difference.

Instruction   Read the following to your class:

> For centuries the Moken people have lived on boats or stilted dwellings along the coast of Burma and Thailand. They make their living deep diving for fish without masks or scuba gear. They are often born, live and die on their boats. The children learn to go diving for fish at an early age. The Moken children can typically dive thirty feet underwater. They learn to lower their heart rate so they can stay under water twice as long as most swimmers. They can see perfectly clearly underwater without goggles. They have learned to change their focus through muscularly changing the shape of the eye's lens when underwater. In the past, seeing clearly underwater was thought to be impossible for the human eye. After discovering these people, others have trained their eyes to see clearly underwater.[18]

Either in small groups, or as a class, discuss the following questions:
1. How is this possible?
2. Why is this important to us?

The science behind this is as follows:

> "Anna Gislén ventured to Thailand's Surin islands where she conducted underwater tests on Moken children and compared their scores with those of European kids vacationing in the area. . . . Gislén found no differences in the children's respective eye structures or in their vision on land. Underwater, however, it was a different story. The Moken children displayed underwater vision twice as sharp as their European counterparts.
>
> Their secret lies in the way their eyes adapt to the underwater environment. The refractive power of the eye's corneal surface, a key to clear vision, is greatly reduced underwater. The different densities of air and water cause the problem. Water has similar density to fluids inside the eye, so refraction is limited as light passes into the eye.
>
> But the Moken are able to accommodate, or muscularly change the shape of the eye's lens, in order to increase light refraction. 'It seems they have learned to control their accommodative response, such that they can voluntarily accommodate even in the blurry underwater environment,' Gislén explained. 'Normally, severe blur does not elicit accommodation, and no accommodative response can be found in untrained European children.' The Moken's pupils also adapt, constricting to a mere 0.08 inch (1.96 millimeters). The European children's pupils constricted to only a tenth of an inch (2.5 millimeters)."[19]

Your students can view this for themselves on YouTube, "How Moken children see with amazing clarity underwater".[20]

If your class does not arrive here by itself, let them know that the brain changed the muscles in the eye to allow the Moken people to do this.

This is important because it proves that our brains can and do change to meet the needs of the environment in which we live. A large limiting factor to brain change can be our own doubt. We learned last class about perspective. If the Moken had the perspective that they could only hold their breath for 30 seconds, they would come up for air every 30 seconds and would have never learned the full extent of what was possible. In today's lesson, we will discuss how our brains can change, and that with this perspective, we can promote positive brain change all throughout life.

You probably don't need to go deep into the sea to dive for fish, but there are many things in your life that are important for your success that have to do with changing your brain. These include things you need to learn and know, such as ways of dealing with people, physical skills, thought patterns, responses to issues, emotional reactivity, and impulse control.

DISCUSSION

List some examples of changes that you or others your age might want to make. (List on the board as students give answers. Expected answers might be improved basketball skills, ability to play an instrument, learn a language, be happier, get along with people better, get better grades, be less anxious, do better in math class, etc.)

After the list is complete, ask how many of these things have to do with changing the brain. The answer should be all of them, but you may have to explain this a bit for students to get it. (For example, you could say, "People's experience so far in life has wired the brain in a certain way. The brain can be rewired through hard work and repetition in amazing ways.")

PLASTICITY

The brain's ability to change is called plasticity. Much of the following information is adapted from the Neurosequential Model of Therapeutics (NMT) and the Neurosequential Model of Education (NME) developed by the ChildTrauma Academy.[21]

Our brains control everything we do. What we think, how we act, how we react, and what we hope and dream all trace back to our brain, and can all be changed. Most people understand changing the brain at a basic level. You know you can learn a new language, and you may even be able to recognize that as you learn this language, you are changing your brain, but these changes can apply to more complex things as well. In fact, there are many accounts of people who lost the ability to speak, walk, use their arms, etc., and they retrained their brains to allow them to do those things again.

Let's take a look at what plasticity looks like at different ages. The plasticity or changeability of the brain is not limited to critical windows or any specific age span. Although the brain is most easily changed early in life, it is still very plastic during adolescence and remains plastic all through life.

"Plasticity is the process through which the outside world gets inside us and changes us. If experiences did not actually change the brain, we would never be able to remember anything."[22]

LAURENCE STEINBERG

CHILDHOOD

When you are born, your brain has already developed the 86 billion brain cells, called neurons, it will need throughout life. The neurons are not yet mature and need to be activated and form connections with other neurons. Experiences cause these neurons to connect with other neurons. Repeated experiences allow connections to become strong pathways, permanently etched into the brain. Infrequent experiences may result in the loss of developing pathways.

By the age of 8 months, an infant living in a safe and loving environment will have formed 500 trillion of these connections. By age two this infant has formed 1000 trillion connections. By the time a child is three years old, the brain structure and design which provides the foundation for future functioning is almost complete. These first few years of life are a time of rapid growth as a child encounters an infinite number of new experiences.

As your brain continues to develop throughout childhood, it has the potential to do almost anything. The development during this time becomes less about physical growth and more about deciding which neurons will stay, which will leave, and where the neural connections need to be strengthened or developed.

ADOLESCENCE

During the adolescent years, there is a period of intense brain rewiring and activity. Your brain is fine tuning and zeroing in on what is most important as you prepare for adulthood. It is getting rid of neurons that are not being used and making the pathways for those that are being used faster and faster. This is a fantastic time of life and you are getting smarter and quicker at the things that matter most to you. You are also losing neurons as your brain prunes those neurons that are not being used.

It is important to make sure you are exercising all parts of your brain during this time and using all the connections that are important to you now and will be important in the future. For example, if you played an instrument throughout most of your childhood and keep at it, you will likely find your skills greatly improve throughout adolescence. This is because your brain has streamlined the connections, allowing you to react more quickly and efficiently.

ADULTHOOD

Some people seem to believe that the brain does not change much later in life. This could not be further from the truth. The brain is a remarkable organ that can grow and change through adulthood. Although the brain is more plastic and easier to change during the early years of life, with repetition of new information or experiences, the brain can continue to learn and develop throughout life.

HOW TO CHANGE THE BRAIN

Changing the brain is very simple in concept, and very challenging in practice. In order to change any specific area of the brain, that area or pathway needs to be activated in a patterned, repetitive manner. Future lessons will discuss the differences in activating the various levels of the brain. For now, what you need to know is that your brain changes by doing a new thing over and over again. While this sounds easy enough, think about some of the things we talked about changing, such as how you respond to things or people, your mood, your impulsivity, etc. In order to change these pathways, each time something occurs that would trigger you to follow old patterns, you need to force yourself to stop, think, and react differently. It will be very hard at first, but with time it will become easier.

Perhaps the best way to understand this is to think of a path through a thick forest. If you are trying to get across the forest, the quickest route is the one that already exists. By default, you will always take that cleared path, and it is quite easy. Now, imagine you wanted to create a new path. You get your machete and start clearing the path. It takes a long time, and there are probably days that you get frustrated and turn back to the previously cleared path. Once you are all the way through, it is still not as clear as the initial path. But, with time, two things will occur. The more you travel this new path, the quicker and easier to travel it becomes. Also, since you are not walking on the initial path, it becomes overgrown and less tempting to walk over.

Our brains work in this same way. Picking the new method is harder, and at times you will begin to move in the right direction, then give up and go back to your default. However, with time, new connections are made in your brain. Choosing the new neural pathway will become easier, and the old neural pathway, if not used, will become less tempting and more difficult to use.

ACTIVITY

Hand each student a piece of paper and lead them through origami or folding an airplane. Record how long it takes to get through to the finished product. Then, have them unfold it, and do it again. Record the time it takes them to re-fold it. You can do this a couple times and record how long it takes each time. The amount of time it takes should go down each time, as it gets easier and easier.

This is how the brain works. Each time you do something, the folds/pathways get more defined, and the action becomes easier. This is why people say, "practice makes perfect." The truth is, really, that practice makes perfect only if you are practicing something the right way. If you folded the paper the wrong way the first time, it made things more difficult and it would have been easier to start with a new piece of paper.

In the same way, practice can solidify good or bad habits. If you learn a skill the wrong way and practice it that way, it later takes much more work to change the bad habit and to do it the right way. Doing anything, including the wrong thing, again and again can make the action become automatic. This is why it's difficult to break bad habits. Once something becomes a habit or routine, it goes into a part of the brain that we cannot consciously control. It takes a lot of repetition to replace bad habits with good ones. This is the downside of plasticity.

"All parts of the brain can modify their functioning in response to specific, repetitive patterns of activation."[23]

BRUCE D. PERRY

Because repeated activation of any part of the brain changes the brain, you can experience changes you do not want when bad things happen or bad choices are made over and over again. In upcoming lessons, we will learn how repeated stress influences the brain and how you can alleviate stress and the damage it can cause. It is also important to note that repeated use of drugs and alcohol will bring about changes in the chemical structure of the brain that can have long-lasting impact.

AN EXAMPLE OF PLASTICITY

When you learn to ride a bike, you are using all parts of your brain, but much of this learning centers in the lower regions, which control balance and large and small muscle movement. Bike riding becomes a motor memory because it is not something that resides in the higher regions of your brain where it can be explained with words. Since muscle movement resides mostly in the lower brain, it is harder to change than information that resides in the top parts of your brain. You can stop riding a bike for many years and you will still remember how to do it. But, what if you tried to ride a different kind of bike? Can you change the learning that occurred?

On YouTube there is a man named Destin Sandlin who had a bike built to go the opposite way that the handlebars were turning.[24] If you turned the handlebars right, the bike went left. If you turned the handlebars left, the bike went right. This seems simple to remember and many people think they will be able to ride this bike just because they understand, in the thinking part of the brain, which way to turn the handlebars. It is almost impossible to ride this bike for anyone at first. The motor memory pathway of riding a regular bike is too strong. Sandlin worked on learning to ride this bike for 8 months and was finally able to do it. It took tons of repetitive practice, but in time, he was able to ride this bike. This proves that the brain can change even deep-seated motor memories. After learning to ride this bike, he found it difficult to ride a regular bike. It took several tries, but in time, he was able to ride a regular bike again. Seeing Sandlin ride this bike is a great example of how, with time, people can change their brain and their unwanted habits or reactions. The example of the backwards bicycle can give students hope.

With time, effort, and practice, it is possible to change your learning even in the lower parts of your brain, but it takes many repetitions for the new experience to take hold. This will be the same with strong relational memories set into your brain early in life regarding attachment and trust, as well as many problem behaviors with learning and managing emotions that can be set early in life. The backwards bike is a great example of the difficulty in changing pathways lower in the brain, but also that it is, in fact, possible. You can change your brain to ride a backwards bike as well as to change any of the unwanted behaviors or approaches you learned early in life. You will need safety and consistent repetition to change these things, but they can change.

ADDITIONAL EXAMPLES OF PLASTICITY

There are many other stories that exemplify brain plasticity. A great book and resource for this is *The Brain That Changes Itself*, by Norman

The backwards bike is a great example of the difficulty in changing pathways lower in the brain, but also that it is, in fact, possible.

Doidge. Find and choose stories that will connect with your students. Some possibilities are listed below:

- In 2006, researchers led by Arne May looked at brains of medical students while studying for exams. MRIs showed that brains increased in grey matter on both sides while studying, and there were areas that continued to grow and increase three months after the exam. This proves that studying can change your brain and increase your intelligence.[25]

- Search on YouTube for "Brain Plasticity, the story of Jody." Jody is a young girl who had half of her brain removed and was able to recover and lead a normal life. Her left hemisphere had such plasticity it was able to take over everything the right hemisphere had done.[26]

- TED Talk by Barbara Arrowsmith-Young: "The Woman Who Changed her Brain."[27] In this talk Barbara Arrowsmith-Young talks about the brain and how she was able to change hers. She was identified in first grade as having a mental block and not being able to learn like other children. She couldn't tell time, understand language, comprehend relationships, or control the left side of her body. Even though she was told it was impossible to change, she found a way. She learned about neural plasticity and found a way to exercise her brain to strengthen the weak areas. By creating exercises for each weak area of her brain she was able to conquer each problem area as she changed her brain.[33]

- In the book, The Brain That Changes Itself, Norman Doidge shares a story about neuroscientist Paul Bach-y-Rita's understanding of brain plasticity after his father had a disabling stroke in 1959. After his stroke, Mr. Bach-y-Rita's face and half his body were paralyzed and he was left unable to speak. The family was told there was no hope of recovery and the father would need to spend the rest of his life in an institution. After their father spent four weeks in rehabilitation with no results, Paul's brother, George, took their father home and began to work with him as he would work with a young child. He began with encouraging crawling and playing games on the floor, throwing balls or marbles and having his father pick them up. Mr. Bach-y-Rita went from crawling, to moving on his knees, to standing, and then to walking. His speech gradually came back. At the end of the year, his recovery was complete enough that he was able to resume teaching full time and traveling. He died at the age of 72 while mountain climbing. When examining his brain after death, it was evident that in spite of catastrophic damage to the brainstem and cortex, the brain had completely reorganized itself to recover functions based on the work George had done.[28]

Reflection **FOCUSING MINDFULNESS EXERCISE**
Introduce the mindfulness exercise:

> Today our mindfulness exercise will be helping you focus on an external object. Your ability to focus is like a muscle that can grow and develop. This is because of your brain's plasticity. It is easy to go

through life in a mindless way because there is so much happening around us and we are busy. Today we will take a few minutes just to be mindful of this object in my hand to work on increasing and fine tuning your focus. Clap when the object reaches its greatest height.

Choose a small object that you can toss into the air. Have the students watch you carefully and clap when the object reaches its greatest height. Do this several times until all students are clapping at close to the same time. Throw the object up at different heights to keep things interesting. If you use an item that can also bounce, change things up by asking students to clap right as it touches the floor. Once they are clapping in unison, add both directions together. Clapping for both directions requires a bit more focus and will add a greater challenge to this activity.

Journal

Make sure each student has a journal and have art supplies available. Let students know journaling is their time to reflect and apply information learned in whatever way works for them. They can use words, colors, drawing or doodling.

Adverse Childhood Experiences

4

Adverse Childhood Experiences

Objectives
& Materials

STUDENTS WILL BE ABLE TO:
- Summarize the basics of the ACE Study
- Understand the possible health impact of adverse childhood experiences
- Discuss the impact of trauma
- Recognize that trauma can impact people differently
- Review interventions or changes to help alleviate stress

MATERIALS:
- Two bottles of seltzer water
- ACES questions

▶ INSTRUCTORS NOTE: This can be a difficult topic for those who have experienced significant adverse childhood experiences (ACE). It is important to handle this topic carefully depending on the class makeup. If you choose the optional activity where students take the ACES survey, make sure you take the survey yourself first. Be careful to set a safe environment and allow students to keep their results private. This lesson must be infused with lots of hope and positivity. This information, when handled with sensitivity and hope, can help students recognize that they are not alone and that what happened to them is not their fault. Most importantly, it can give them hope and motivation to begin dealing with the effects of adverse childhood experiences in their life. Never lose sight of the fact that this information can also be disturbing. Go slow, and skip parts if necessary. Make sure you are taking the time to process any feelings and concerns that come up.

Making
Connections

The following activity is adapted from the trauma training designed by Diane Wagenhals of the Lakeside Global Institute.[29] Have two bottles of seltzer water that look exactly the same. Before class starts shake one bottle vigorously. Ask the students what they see and what is the same or different about the bottles. Ideally, they will see no differences.

After all students have had the opportunity to observe and reply, open the non-shaken bottle and pour some into a glass. Then open the shaken bottle, and be prepared for a little mess. Discuss with the students the fact that we cannot always tell what is going on beneath the surface with people, just like we couldn't see what had happened to this bottle. The experiences that people have faced have an impact, even if it is not visible to us. Sometimes it takes an explosion for us to realize there is something that has gone wrong. Share the following with your students:

> Last class we learned about brain plasticity and the fact that the brain can change. Today we are going to learn about how trauma and adverse childhood experiences can change the brain. The only difference between the two bottles of water was one experience right before you came in the classroom, but that was enough to change everything. (Take the first bottle and shake it up again.) Now this bottle has had an adverse experience. What would happen if I opened it up? I am not going to open it, yet. The goal for today is to work through understanding the potential impact of adverse experiences, but also recognizing that we can take control over how it impacts us.

Preparing the Brain

ENERGY BREATHING

Introduce the breathing exercise:

> Before we learn some new things about brain plasticity, we are going to do a breathing exercise to prepare your brain to be calm and alert so it can take in the new information. Has anyone been practicing breathing exercises at home? How is it going? (If students have examples to share, take some time to listen to how it is going.) Today we will do another new breathing exercise. Record your heart rate before and after to see what impact this breathing exercise has on your heart rate and your brainstem.
>
> Take a long breath in while rubbing your hands together vigorously to a count of six. Then breathe out, while tapping the tips of your fingers together. Count slowly as you do this to a count of six in and six out. Repeat this for a minute or two. (Instructors, you are working to slowly build up the time students are able to do a breathing exercise.)
>
> Adapted from *Doodles, Dances and Ditties*[30]

Instruction

THE IMPACT OF ADVERSE EXPERIENCES

As we have been learning, your brain is plastic and makes changes based on input and experiences. It is important to understand that our brains can change both for better and for worse. What you do and what you experience impacts your brain. When bad things happen, your brain is impacted just as it is when good input is received.

Today we are going to look at how adverse experiences early in life can change your brain. It is important to understand this because you have the power to change this impact if you know what to do about it. Understanding why you think, feel, or do the things you do can be helpful if you want to make changes.

Research has shown that early adverse experiences can have a tremendous impact on your future and your health if the physiological changes in your brain and body are not dealt with. The impact includes your physical health, mental health, academic achievements, and impulse control. The good news is that all of these things can be addressed with interventions that target the appropriate areas of the brain.

ACEs is a very important study that you may have never heard about. Most people haven't. It was developed in the late 1990s by Dr. Robert Anda and Dr. Vincent Felitti.[31] It has been ongoing since then. ACE stands for the Adverse Childhood Experiences Study.

Over 17,000 adults in the suburbs of San Diego volunteered to participate in this initial study. These adults were asked ten questions which focused on common types of childhood trauma. Five of these questions dealt with things that happened to them such as physical, sexual, or emotional abuse, and physical or emotional neglect. The other five questions dealt with things that happened to parents or other household members such as abuse, divorce, mental illness, suicide, alcoholism, or imprisonment. The answers to these ten questions determined their ACE score.

This study is important because it showed how incredibly common adverse childhood experiences are.

- 2 out of 3 people have at least one ACE
- 1 out of 5 people have at least three ACEs
- 1 out of 8 people had at four or more ACEs

The study also showed that increased ACE scores correlated with an increased risk for some significant health-related issues across the lifespan including cancer, heart disease, depression, drug addiction, and suicide. Until this point, no one had studied how repetitive and stressful childhood situations can affect people over the course of their lives. Exposure to early adversity affects the brain and body. High doses of adversity affect brain structure and function. For those with high ACE scores, there were changes throughout the brain that impacted thinking, decision making, cortisol levels, stress hormones, the immune system, and the fear response.

If you have a high ACE score, it is important to recognize that you are not alone. Many people have had adverse experiences. The first step in combatting the negative impact of adverse experiences is to recognize the cause. The cause is things that have happened to you, not decisions you have made or things you have done. You cannot change what happened to you, but you can take charge by changing your brain for the better moving forward.

ACE scores are not a destiny but a tool for understanding your own risk. This knowledge can empower you to make changes that can lessen the

//"What's predictable is preventable."[31]

ROBERT ANDA

impact of adverse experiences and toxic stress. The good news is that with knowledge comes power. You don't have to be at the mercy of the stress these experiences create.

In this course, you will learn how to alleviate the impact of adverse experiences on the brain and therefore the body. Repetitive and ongoing adversity in early childhood has been called toxic stress. This stress can change your brain over time and increase your chances of developing health issues if it is not addressed. Because your brain, as you have learned, is plastic and continually changing in response to its environment, you can take steps to undo many of the changes caused by early childhood adversity.

There is well documented research[34] that shows how your brain and body can become healthier through things you do and the relationships you have. You will learn many ways throughout this course to undo the damaging impact of early childhood adversity and stress on your brain and your life. With recognition of the issues and work towards positive brain change, you can ensure that you are in the percentage of people whose health is not negatively impacted by their ACE score.

In addition to the ten adverse experiences covered in this study, some people have experienced other forms of trauma such as automobile accidents, fire, crimes, shootings, medical trauma, or the injury or death of a parent or other loved one. These experiences may have similar effects if it happened during early childhood.

Another experience that can have a negative impact on health and brain development is neglect. "Neglect" means that an experience needed for brain development at a certain age was missed. This can include emotional and physical neglect as well as missing social, physical, educational, and relational experiences. As a result of missing experiences, the part of the brain that needed these experiences was not able to fully develop or complete the building of neural pathways. The brain is therefore developmentally behind in certain areas.

The impact of adversity and neglect is going to be very different from person to person. One of the key factors is the age at which the trauma or neglect occurred. Whatever region of the brain that is developing at the time of trauma or neglect is the region that will be most impacted. And of course, since we are each different, we will react to trauma or neglect in our own unique ways.

While the seltzer bottle analogy is not perfect, it does begin to create a good picture of the impact of trauma on the brain. The truth is, we all basically look the same on the outside. We do not carry around a badge that shows our ACE score or explains our darkest moments in life. Instead, most people put on a pretty good act until something pushes them too far. People who have had adverse experiences are often oversensitized to stress and may therefore react more strongly to additional stress. When people are pushed too far, their reaction is often to explode, either outwardly or inwardly. For the seltzer bottle, exploding really only happens one way, but for humans, exploding can take on many different styles. Some people act out by yelling, cursing, hitting, or breaking things. Some people freeze; some may withdraw

"There are people with high ACE scores who do remarkably well. Resilience builds throughout life and close relationships are key."[33]

JACK SHONKOFF

or flee. Even within these examples, there are many ways to react in your own individual style. There is no manual for how people who have had adverse experiences are going to react or respond to different situations.

The good news is that it is never too late to make a positive impact on our brains. If you believe you have experienced some of the ACEs listed above, or some other types of trauma or neglect, chances are that your brain has been impacted. This impact can play out differently for different people. Some results could be poor academic achievement, depression, lack of impulse control, health issues, alcoholism, and acting out behaviors. In upcoming lessons, we will take a closer look at how the brain develops and how to begin to bring healing to the lower regions of the brain, which may be impacted by early childhood trauma and/or neglect. In the meantime, practice the breathing and mindfulness exercises you have been doing in class. This is a great first step towards promoting a healthy brain.

One important thing to know about changing your brain is the importance of maintaining hope. Research has shown that hope has the unbelievable power to keep us pushing through some of the most unimaginable circumstances. Finding bits of hope that you can hold onto will help you push through problems in unbelievable ways.

DISCUSSION
- What are some things or people in your life that give you hope?
- What are some possible ways to increase hope?

Share the following summary with students:

> If you need help in processing any trauma or adverse experiences, talk to a counselor. Your brain can change, but this change will be a lot easier with a trained professional helping you through it. (At this point, take the seltzer bottle you shook up and slowly open it and shut it several times, letting air out and a little seltzer, without letting it completely explode all over.) A trained and caring person can help you to process and release what is locked up inside of you. This does not mean it will always be easy, and it still may get messy at times, but it will hopefully help you avoid any explosions like we saw at the beginning of class that impacted a wide array of people.

OPTIONAL ACTIVITY
For those who want to see or take the actual ACE questionnaire, you can download it from Acestoohigh.com. Make sure that if you have students take this survey, you leave ample time to process it with them afterwards and have time or resources available for anyone that needs a private conversation.

> "Psychologists say that having a grandparent who loves you, a teacher who understands and believes in you, or a trusted friend you can confide in may mitigate the long-term effects of early trauma."[35]

DANNY DE BELIUS

Reflection **MINDFUL EATING**

Give each student a piece of candy and ask them to wait to unwrap or eat it until the exercise begins. Before doing the exercise, discuss the importance of noticing sensations. Being mindful of sensations can help an individual focus and calm down. Introduce the mindfulness exercise:

You do a lot of things automatically, without even thinking about it. Things like brushing your teeth, tying your shoes, or making yourself breakfast each day become so routine that you can go through the motions without putting any thought into what you are doing.

This exercise is to help you be more mindful – aware of your experiences and how your body is feeling in a given moment. We often eat candy without even thinking about it or fully enjoying the experience. If your mind wanders, don't allow yourself to get frustrated. Everyone's mind wanders. Don't judge yourself. This is something that takes practice. When you notice your mind wandering, just gently bring it back to the taste of the candy in your mouth. The more you are aware and pay attention to what your mind is doing, the more you can control. If you are not aware of what you are doing, it is more difficult to control it. It is also difficult to be anxious about the future if your mind is focused on the present.

Read the following script slowly with long pauses. Play soft, calming music in the background.

Take the candy. Feel the weight and texture in your hand. Smell the candy. What is your body's reaction to the smell? Can you feel an increase of saliva? Put the candy in your mouth. What is the flavor? Let it roll around on your tongue. What does it taste like? Is it a strong taste? Pay attention to your mouth and continue to focus on the candy. What is its texture—is it smooth or rough? Can you taste it in different parts of your mouth? Be aware of how it feels on your tongue as it rolls around in your mouth. Be aware of this experience—is the candy enjoyable to eat? Is it getting smaller? What is happening to the texture? Continue to be aware of all of your senses in relation to the candy and we will sit quietly and be mindful for a little while longer.

After a few seconds, ask if anyone would like to share how the experience was for them. What did they notice?

Journal

Make sure each student has a journal and have art supplies available. Let students know journaling is their time to reflect and apply information learned in whatever way works for them. They can use words, colors, drawing or doodling.

ADDITIONAL RESOURCES:

- Berk, N. (2015, February 17). How childhood trauma affects health across a lifetime. Retrieved at https://www.youtube.com/watch?v=95ovIJ3dsNk
- www.acestoohigh.com

Calm/Alert

Alarm

Fear

Terror

Brain State

5

Recognizing Brain Regions

Recognizing Brain Regions

Objectives & Materials

STUDENTS WILL BE ABLE TO:
- Review the concept of brain plasticity
- Recognize the four brain regions
- Compare and contrast the roles played by each region of the brain

MATERIALS:
- Wood blocks or other building material
- Student workbooks or brain region worksheet
- Visuals for each brain region
- Plastic objects for brain plasticity

Making Connections

INTRODUCE THE LESSON:
As we learned in the last two lessons, the brain is changeable or has plasticity. (Show plastic objects as a visual reminder.) Not all parts of the brain have the same degree of plasticity, some are more easily changed than others. In a minute you will have a chance to make your best guess and discuss which area of the brain you think is most easily changeable.

ACTIVITY
Label 1-4 with 1 being the hardest to change and 4 being most easily changeable.

_____ Part that controls heart, breathing and temperature

_____ Part that controls muscle movement and fine motor skills

_____ Part that controls relationships and emotions

_____ Part that controls learning and taking in new information

Post these four statements around the room. Ask students to move around the room depending on how they numbered each one. Have them move to their #1 statement. Have students discuss with the others in their group why they made this #1. Then, have them share with the larger group. They can change their answers as they go if they are swayed by what they hear. Next they can move to their #2 statement. Do this through each of the statements.

Discuss why it might be a good thing that certain parts of the brain are more difficult to change than others. When the students are done, give them the right answers, along with the name of each brain part. Explain that in this lesson we will learn about these four parts of the brain. (Answers: brainstem #1, midbrain #2, limbic #3, cortex #4.)

Preparing the Brain

SIX-SECOND BREATHING
Adapted from *Doodles, Dances and Ditties*[36]

Demonstrate the exercise for the students, then invite them to participate. Stand with your arms at your sides. Breathe in as you slowly lift your arms out to the side and above your head (like wings) to a count of six. Then slowly lower your arms down to your sides at a count of six. Repeat this exercise for two to four minutes. This exercise is good for relaxing students who need to be calmed, and for increasing energy for students who need to wake up. Either way, it will help prepare the students to take in new information.

Instruction

The information in this chapter is based on the Neurosequential Model of Therapeutics (NMT) and the Neurosequential Model of Education (NME) developed by the ChildTrauma Academy.[37] We will be using a simple model of the brain that divides the brain into four regions.

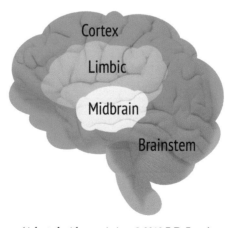

(Adapted with permission, © 2012 B.D. Perry)

The brain is much more complex than this picture, but this picture is a great tool to help you understand and remember how your brain functions. The brain develops from the bottom up. Different parts develop at different ages. Positive and negative experiences impact whatever area of the brain is developing at that time.

BRAINSTEM

The brainstem is the first part of the brain to develop. It develops first because it is needed to regulate our most basic survival needs. It is located at the bottom of the brain above the neck. The brainstem develops almost completely while a baby is in utero.

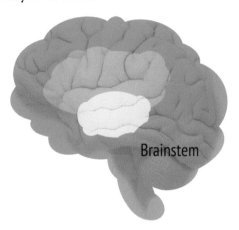

(Adapted with permission, © 2012 B.D. Perry)

The brainstem is responsible for the life-sustaining functions, such as regulating:

- Heart rate
- Body temperature
- Breathing
- Blood pressure

These functions are often unconscious. We don't spend time thinking about how to breathe or regulate our heart rate, blood pressure, or temperature. They happen automatically. The brainstem is very sensitive to signals of fear, distress, and danger. Because it is reflexive, it can change instantaneously in response to stress signals in our environment. To help students remember, there are visuals for each brain region to use as reminders throughout these lessons. The visual for the brainstem will be a stethoscope (or thermometer or whatever you choose).

In the beginning of today's lesson, we learned that the part of the brain that controls heart rate, breathing, and temperature is the hardest to change. This is the brainstem. It is a good thing the brainstem is hard to change, because you wouldn't want something to be able to easily change these life-sustaining functions. But with that said, the brainstem can change for the better or worse, like any other part of your brain. It will just take a little more time and effort.

ACTIVITY

Have students take a moment to fill in the brain in their workbooks, indicating what they just learned about the brainstem.

The brainstem is reflexive. It can change instantaneously in response to stress signals in the environment.

MIDBRAIN

The second part of the brain to develop is the midbrain. This is connected to the brainstem and develops in the early years of childhood. The midbrain is responsible for the following:

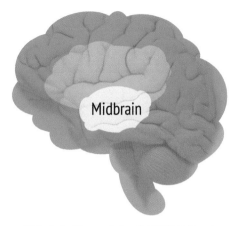

(Adapted with permission, © 2012 B.D. Perry)

- Fine motor skills
- Large motor skills
- Movement and balance

The midbrain is reactive, not thinking or feeling. The midbrain is often called the reptilian brain because this is where the brain of reptiles stops growing. Reptiles are mostly reactive and reflexive without emotions, or emotional connections. Because of this, we will be visually representing the midbrain with an alligator.

If your students would be interested in more examples, the midbrain is also responsible for the following reflexive actions:
- Appetite
- Salivation, swallowing
- Sleep
- Directing sense impulses throughout the body
- Maintaining equilibrium
- Sense of smell and taste
- Eye movement
- Hearing

ACTIVITY

Have students take a moment to fill in the brain in their workbooks, indicating what they just learned about the midbrain.

LIMBIC SYSTEM

The third part of the brain to develop is the limbic system. The limbic system is located in the middle of the brain. It continues developing through adolescence.

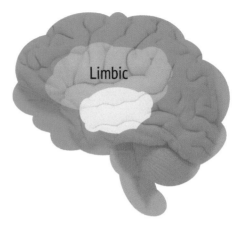

(Adapted with permission, © 2012 B.D. Perry)

The limbic system is responsible for:
- Relationships
- Emotional reactivity
- Short-term memory

We will be representing the limbic system visually by a heart for emotions and relationships.

▶ INSTRUCTOR'S NOTE: The limbic system is also responsible for sexual behavior, but this may be more of a distraction than help to your students. It is your choice whether to include it or not.

ACTIVITY

Have students take a moment to fill in the brain in their workbooks, indicating what they just learned about the limbic system.

CORTEX

Lastly, the cortex sits on the top of the brain. It continues to develop through adulthood. It is the most plastic and complex part of the brain. It is where thinking and judgment reside. The cortex is responsible for:
- Abstract thought
- Concrete thought
- Verbal and non-verbal communication

We will be visually representing the cortex by a chess piece (or reading glasses, book, etc.) to represent the higher level thinking and communication.

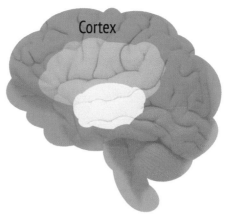

Cortex

(Adapted with permission, © 2012 B.D. Perry)

The cortex is also responsible for the following: (Feel free to add whatever is helpful to your students.)

- Judgment
- Problem solving ability
- Insight/self-awareness
- Self-image
- Reading and writing
- Ability to modulate and control behavior
- Mathematical reasoning

ACTIVITY

Have students take a moment to fill in the brain in their workbooks, indicating what they just learned about the cortex.

ALL PARTS OF THE BRAIN WORK TOGETHER

When traumatic events have impacted the lower regions of the brain, all areas are impacted. Information must filter through the bottom areas of the brain in order to get to the cortex. If the bottom areas are overdeveloped due to stress and/or if the cortex is underdeveloped, the ability of the cortex to modulate or control the impulses coming from these lower regions can be significantly impaired.

ACTIVITY:

Have students build a tower with wood blocks or some other type of building material. Afterwards discuss the strategy for building a strong tower. Note how everyone started at the bottom and how the bottom had to be strong and stable in order to support the top parts of the tower. Talk about how hard or easy it is to make changes after the tower is built. Can you pull blocks out of the bottom and make changes to it easily? Note how much easier it is to make changes to the top. Talk about the similarities to the different parts of the brain. If you have time, you can color or label the blocks to represent each brain part.

> The cortex continues to develop through adulthood. It is the most plastic and complex part of the brain. It is where thinking and judgment reside.

Reflection   LEAVES FLOATING ON A STREAM

The following exercise is an adaptation of a classic. Many authors and clinicians provide versions of this mindfulness practice. We will be using it to help students be mindful of all functions from all areas of their brains: sensations, muscle tension, emotions, and thoughts.

The main purpose is to sit back and observe thoughts, emotions, and sensations rather than to get caught up in them. These things come and go like leaves floating down a stream. We don't need to react to them, just notice them. Introduce the mindfulness exercise:

Imagine yourself sitting next to a stream. You can close your eyes if you are comfortable, or focus on a spot on your desk or the floor. Imagine each sense. What does the stream look like? What do you smell? What do you hear? Can you feel anything? The spray of water? A cool breeze? (Don't rush this. Allow time for students to visualize each sense.) If you have trouble imagining the stream, it is okay. Follow along with this exercise, it will work either way. Bring your attention to your breath. Focus on breathing in and out. What is the temperature of the air you are breathing in.? Does it change as it goes through your body? Continue to breathe in and out. With each breath out, imagine any tension leaving your body. Notice your muscles one at a time from your feet to your head and relax them as you breathe out.

Now begin to notice any emotions you may be feeling or thoughts you are thinking. Some emotions or thoughts may rush by and some may linger. Simply allow yourself to notice them. As you begin to notice thoughts or emotions, imagine putting those words on a leaf and letting it float by. Just let the thoughts and emotions come and watch them drift by. If any thoughts or emotions stop, keep focusing on the water flowing by. Your attention may wander. Painful thoughts or emotions may surface. You may begin to feel uncomfortable or think this exercise is "stupid." You may get stuck replaying a thought. That's okay. It is what our minds do. Continue to gently bring your focus back to your thoughts and emotions and place them on a leaf that is floating by. Now bring your attention back to your breath. Focus on your breathing for a moment. When you are ready, open your eyes or look up.

Journal

Make sure each student has a journal and have art supplies available. Let students know journaling is their time to reflect and apply information learned in whatever way works for them. They can use words, colors, drawing or doodling.

CHAPTER 6

Brainstem

6

Brainstem

Objectives & Materials

STUDENTS WILL BE ABLE TO:
- Understand that the brainstem is the first part of the brain to develop
- Review the areas the brainstem controls
- Practice activities that activate the brainstem
- Recognize signs of brainstem dysregulation
- Determine activities that help regulate the brainstem

Materials:
- Brain chart with brainstem filled in
- Pictures of babies using senses
- Visual item for brainstem
- Items for calming activities
- Water bottles and straws

Making Connections

In previous lessons we have been talking about the brain's plasticity and the various parts of the brain. Any time you learn something new, that is your brain changing. If you meet a new person and remember their name, that is a new fact in your brain. If you talked with them and developed a connection, that is a new relationship. If you learned a new skateboard trick, that is a new motor skill.

Have students write down an example of a way their brain has changed since the last class. (You may want to change the time frame depending what you think will work best.) Have students share what they wrote and put their answers on the board. After the answers are on the board, ask the class what part of the brain they think would be most involved for each answer. Note that the entire brain is involved in learning, but certain parts are most responsible. For example, learning a new fact would be the cortex, learning about or developing a relationship would be the limbic system, and motor skills would be mid-brain. Probably very little would be brainstem, but if they practiced breathing exercises or calmed themselves down by their senses that would involve the brainstem. Use your brain region visuals as you refer to each area of the brain to help students remember. Some answers might involve multiple parts of the brain. For instance, playing a team sport, losing your temper and apologizing to teammates could be mid-brain, limbic, and cortex. The discussion and review of what each part of the brain is responsible for is what is most important here.

Preparing the Brain

One way to calm yourself down when you are stressed, hyper, anxious, or angry is to use deep breathing to increase oxygen and lower your heart rate. That is why we have been practicing breathing exercises. Deep breathing helps change the brain from the brainstem up. In this lesson, we will use a breathing exercise in the form of a quick review of what the students remember about the brainstem.

Since breathing impacts the brainstem, this exercise uses the breath for a short true/false quiz. Give each student a cotton ball on their desk. Have students blow the cotton ball to the right side of the desk if the question is true (or right) and to the left side of their desk if the answer is false.

- The brainstem regulates your heart rate (T)
- The brainstem is the last part of the brain to develop (F)
- The brainstem is responsible for movement (F)
- Reptiles have a brainstem (T)
- The brainstem regulates your temperature (T)

Instruction

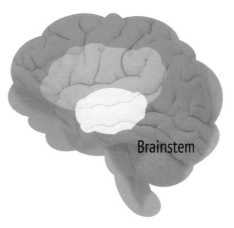

(Adapted with permission, © 2012 B.D. Perry)

Share the correct answer each time.

The information in this chapter is adapted from the Neurosequential Model of Therapeutics (NMT) and the Neurosequential Model of Education (NME) developed by the ChildTrauma Academy. Remember that the brainstem is responsible for the life-sustaining functions such as regulating heart rate, temperature, breathing, and blood pressure. Besides the four areas already discussed, the brainstem also controls metabolism and the ability to pay attention. (Show visual item for brainstem.)

Since the brainstem is the first part of the brain to develop, it develops almost completely while a baby is in utero. If something goes wrong during pregnancy, delivery, or the first few months of life, there may be some areas of the brainstem that are under or overdeveloped. The brainstem can be improved and developed at any time in life but change will happen more quickly the younger the person is.

The brainstem is very sensitive to signals of fear, distress, and danger. Because it is reflexive, it reacts instantaneously in response to stress signals in the environment. It is the hardest part of the brain to change but can still be changed with time and effort.

Some signs of an underdeveloped or overdeveloped brainstem may be: (Note that many people have one or more of these things. They each can be caused by things other than brainstem issues—but if there are strong indicators in a few of these areas, brainstem interventions over time may bring improvement.)

- Abnormally high or low heart rate
- High or low blood pressure
- Breathing problems
- Skin sensitivities
- Abnormal body temperature (high, low, erratic)
- Metabolic problems (eating without gaining weight or gaining weight with little eating)
- Need to chew gum or have something in the mouth often
- Difficulty chewing food or taking pills
- Distractibility, difficulty in focusing
- Difficulty shifting attention from one thing to another

▶ INSTRUCTOR'S NOTE: Choose only the things from this list and the amount of items that you feel your students can handle.

Whether there are brainstem issues present or not, all of us can benefit from knowing, using, and understanding brainstem interventions. Since all information enters the brain through the brainstem, learning to calm your brain through the brainstem can be instrumental to calming yourself down when upset.

INTERVENTIONS

To learn what interventions can help to calm or develop the brainstem, let's think about newborn babies. The things that develop the brainstem mostly happen in utero. Think about the things a baby is experiencing in utero. There is the strong sound and vibrations of the mother's heartbeat. There is a perfect environment where they are never cold or hot, hungry or thirsty. There is the rhythmic movement as the mother walks. There is the surrounding amniotic fluid that keeps the baby protected and safe. When the baby is born, it is a bit of a rude awakening. In order to calm a newborn baby there are many things we do to try to remind them of the sounds, vibrations, and sensations felt during their development in the womb. Since the brainstem is the only part of an infant's brain that is almost fully developed, the things that work to calm an infant have to do with interventions that calm the brainstem.

Have students list some of the things they can think of (show pictures to help if needed). Some students may share odd things they saw their parents do with younger siblings; chances are that the root of those solutions can be found below.

- Rocking
- Bouncing
- Swinging
- Music
- Singing
- Swaddling
- Humming
- Talking in soothing tones
- Something in mouth—pacifier/bottle
- Vibrations (car, washing machine)
- Carrying close to the body
- Caressing

All of these things help to calm and/or develop the brainstem. Once a child is older we may expect them to no longer need these things, but if they had adverse experiences or missed needed experiences early in life, they may need similar interventions to continue calming and developing the brainstem. Let's look at activities that are similar but can be appropriate for older children, teens, and adults.

- Rocking chairs
- Bouncy chairs
- Swings
- Music at the rhythm of a mother's heartbeat
- Clothes or wraps that make you feel secure (fitted, athletic shirts; weighted or other blankets)
- Chewing gum, candy, hard pretzels
- Drinking from a straw
- Chew jewelry or pencil toppers
- Massage
- Deep breathing (babies do this automatically when held and calmed by parent)
- Cuddling with an animal, feeling the warmth, the heartbeat, petting, etc.

Remember, to be able to change any part of the brain, patterned, repetitive activation is needed. It is most helpful in changing the brain if these activities are available and can be repeated for short periods of time throughout the day.

ACTIVITY

Have students experiment with some of these things, checking their heart rate before and after. Have available whatever you can throughout the classroom. Play calming music. Have hard pretzels, hard candy, or chewing gum, and water with straws available. If you have rocking chairs, soft blankets, or hand-held massagers, make them available. Add whatever else you have available from the list above. Spend time allowing students to experience each thing while staying quiet and listening to the music. Encourage them to focus on their breathing throughout the time as well.

Remember, to be able to change any part of the brain, patterned, repetitive activation is needed.

Tell students that in a few minutes they will have time to reflect and journal about what they have learned. In order to give their brains time to reflect and put this information into long-term memory, they will first do another mindfulness exercise.

Reflection

MINDFULNESS EXERCISE

Play soft calming music and give water bottles with a straw. This is a mindfulness activity that focuses on drinking water through a straw. Write your own script, similar to the candy script from the last lesson. Focus on how the water feels coming up the straw, what the muscles in your mouth are doing, the temperature of the water, how the temperature changes as you hold it in your mouth, and how the water feels as it goes down your throat. Think about where it goes next and whether you can feel it move through your body.

After the activity, talk about the benefits of drinking water. The process of drinking helps you slow down and regulate your breathing. When you need a break to calm down, drinking from a bottle of water can be good intervention. It is difficult to cry or yell when drinking water. Water provides essential energy to the brain, keeps the nerve signals going, delivers nutrients to the brain, and removes toxins. Sucking through a straw uses muscles in your mouth that activate the brainstem.

Journal

Make sure each student has a journal and have art supplies available. Let students know journaling is their time to reflect and apply information learned in whatever way works for them. They can use words, colors, drawing or doodling.

Midbrain

7

Midbrain

Objectives
& Materials

STUDENTS WILL BE ABLE TO:
- Recognize the areas the midbrain controls
- Practice activities that activate the midbrain
- Recognize signs of midbrain dysregulation
- Determine activities that help regulate the midbrain

MATERIALS:
- Brain chart with midbrain filled in
- Visual items for brainstem and midbrain

Making
Connections

Movement is helpful to use during a review. This review uses bilateral movement and crossing the midline to help students solidify the information in long-term memory. Have students stand. Instruct them to put their hands on their brainstem if the statement is true and cross their arms if the statement is false.

The brainstem is responsible for:
- Heart rate (T)
- Relationships (F)
- Body temperature (T)
- Breathing (T)
- Blood pressure (T)
- Emotions (F)
- Distractibility (T)
- Movement (F)

Interventions that can calm the brainstem are:

- Rocking (T)
- Swinging (T)
- Calm music (T)
- Punching something (F)
- Petting a dog (T)
- Chewing (T)
- Sports (F)
- Blankets (T)
- Talking (F)

Preparing the Brain

Before we learn about the midbrain, we are going to do a brain break to prepare your brain to be calm and alert so that it can take in the new information. Today we will use figure eight breathing. Large muscle movement impacts the midbrain. Since we will be learning about the midbrain today we will be using this breathing exercise that includes large muscle movement. Record your heart rate before and after to see what impact this breathing exercise has on your heart rate.

FIGURE EIGHT BREATHING
Adapted from the *Brain Gym®* movement, Lazy 8s.[38]

Hold a thumb up about 10–12 inches centered in front of your face. Using this as the center point, draw a sideways figure eight in front of your face with your thumb. Don't move your head but follow your thumb with your eyes. The movement should be slow and controlled, and the figure eight should be 12 to 16 inches wide. Once you have done this a couple times, focus on breathing in as you cross the middle, and then breathe out as you cross the middle again. Repeat this 10–12 times.

Instruction

The information in this chapter is adapted from the Neurosequential Model of Therapeutics (NMT) and the Neurosequential Model of Education (NME) developed by the ChildTrauma Academy.

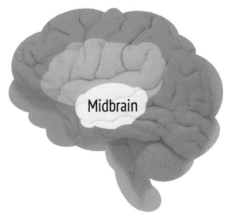

(Adapted with permission, © 2012 B.D. Perry)

Remember that the midbrain is the second part of the brain to develop and is responsible for the following:
* Fine motor skills
* Large motor skills
* Movement and balance

The midbrain is also responsible for:
* Appetite
* Salivation, swallowing
* Sleep
* Directing sense impulses throughout the body
* Maintaining equilibrium
* Sense of smell and taste
* Hearing

The midbrain is reactive, not thinking or feeling. It maintains a person's equilibrium and sends sense impulses throughout the body. Some signs of problems with the midbrain may be: (Note that many people have one or more of these things. They each can be caused by things other than midbrain issues—but if there are strong indicators in some of these areas, midbrain interventions over time may bring improvement).
* Clumsiness (always bumping into things)
* Poor fine motor skills (bad handwriting)
* Sleep problems
* Eating problems
* Impulsivity
* Difficulty with transitions
* Daydreaming
* Self-harm
* Sensory seeking
* Sensory avoidant

Whether the midbrain had problems in development or not, all of us can benefit from knowing, using, and understanding midbrain interventions. All information enters your brain through the brainstem and then goes up through your midbrain. Learning to calm your brain through the brainstem and midbrain can be instrumental to calming yourself down when upset. We already learned physical interventions to regulate the brainstem. Today we will learn interventions for the midbrain.

INTERVENTIONS
To learn what interventions can help to calm or develop the midbrain, let's think about young children. The things that develop the midbrain mostly happen during the infant to toddler years. Young children are learning where their body is in space and how to use their muscles to move and react to their environment. In order to walk, they first need to roll over, then sit up, crawl, etc. They are learning how to use their muscles and their balance.

What are some things you see children doing with their muscles and bodies as they grow and learn to explore the world? Have students list some of the things they can think of (show pictures to help if needed).

- Skipping
- Bouncing
- Jumping
- Building
- Exploring
- Balancing
- Drawing/coloring
- Crafts
- Playing at recess
- Climbing

All of these things involve use of small and large muscles and can help to calm and/or continue development of the midbrain.

ACTIVITY

Heavy muscle work is one of the few interventions that can either calm you down or wake you up, depending on what you need. Let's try some of those activities now. Have the students do some isometric exercises and record their heart rates before and after. Isometric exercises could include chair pushups, pushing palms against each other like you are praying, interlocking fingers and pulling hard without releasing your grip, pushing down on the floor with your legs while sitting in a chair, etc. You will find many more isometric exercises online. Have students discuss what they liked or didn't like about the exercises. What impact, if any, did they notice to their heart rate?

Besides large muscle movement, using your fine motor skills can also be calming to the midbrain. This is why some people like to doodle or color while listening. There is a psychologist named Jackie Andrade who, through research, showed that people who doodled while listening remembered 29% more than those who just listened.[39] Midbrain interventions can include any kind of use of the small muscles in your hands such as fidgeting, building, gardening, arts and crafts, sewing, knitting, etc.

Based on what has been covered so far about large and small muscle movement and balance, have the students list their ideas for some midbrain activities that could be helpful to students their age in calming the midbrain.

Examples of midbrain activities that can be age appropriate for older children and adults:

- Walking
- Weight lifting
- Isometrics
- Creative Arts
- Doodling
- Coloring
- Gardening
- Knitting
- Drumming
- Sports
- Balancing activities
- Standing while you work
- Working with animals

Remember that it is important for activities to be done in a patterned and repetitive manner throughout the day for the greatest effectiveness.

Heavy muscle work is one of the few interventions that can either calm you down or wake you up, depending on what you need.

Reflection   **LARGE AND SMALL MUSCLE MINDFULNESS EXERCISE**

Have movement activities posted around the room such as isometrics, jumping jacks, wall pushups, etc. and fine motor activities on the other side of the room such as building blocks, coloring pages, journals, etc. Have students take their pulse, then try one or more movement activities for at least two full minutes and then one fine motor activity for at least two full minutes. Have students focus on the feelings that occur during each activity and record their pulse before and after.

Journal

Make sure each student has a journal and have art supplies available. Let students know journaling is their time to reflect and apply information learned in whatever way works for them. They can use words, colors, drawing or doodling.

Limbic System

8

Limbic System

Objectives & Materials

STUDENTS WILL BE ABLE TO:
- Recognize signs of limbic system dysregulation
- Determine activities that help develop the limbic system
- Understand how relationships affect the brain
- Reflect on the characteristics of a healthy relationship

MATERIALS:
- Brainstem, midbrain, and limbic visual items

Making Connections

In the previous lessons we learned about the brainstem and midbrain, and interventions that help to regulate each of them. Have students work in groups of two or three to come up with as many interventions as they can remember that can calm or help regulate the brainstem and midbrain. Give time for each group to come up with as many as they can, then make a joint class list on the board. Ask if students have tried any of these things or have been more mindful of things they were already doing from this list.

Preparing the Brain

MIRRORING BREATHING

Introduce the breathing exercise to your students:

Today we are going to do a breathing exercise that includes focusing and mirroring the breathing of another person. Choose a partner and stand back to back, close and almost touching. Choose one person to be the leader. When I say start, the leader should begin doing one of the breathing exercises we have learned. Use your senses to determine to the best of your ability how your leader is breathing and try to breathe with them. The leaders should not try to hide what they are doing and should allow their bodies to move with each breath. Follow along for a few minutes until I say switch. It is okay if you cannot identify and mirror the exact same breathing exercise. Just focus on your breathing and use your senses to feel what is happening around you.

Instruction

The information in this chapter is adapted from the Neurosequential Model of Therapeutics (NMT) and the Neurosequential Model of Education (NME) developed by the ChildTrauma Academy.

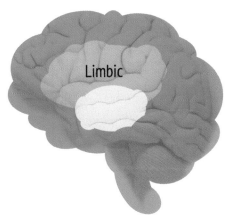

(Adapted with permission, © 2012 B.D. Perry)

Remember that the limbic system is responsible for:
- Relationships
- Emotional reactivity
- Short-term memory

It is also responsible for sexual behavior. (Instructors can decide whether adding this is helpful or distracting to students.)

Some signs of issues in limbic system development may be: (Note that many people have one or more of these things. They each can be caused by things other than limbic system issues—but if there are strong indicators in a few these areas, limbic system interventions over time may bring improvement.)
- Inability to find pleasure in healthy relational interactions
- Unhealthy forms of reward such as over-eating, cutting, drug and alcohol abuse, or promiscuity
- Becoming overly anxious, aggressive or withdrawn when upset
- Taking a long time to calm down when upset or excited (more than 15 minutes)
- Difficulty reading the verbal or non-verbal cues of others
- Selfish or inconsiderate behavior towards others
- Having few age-appropriate friendships
- Needing repetition of simple directions

Whether there are limbic system issues or not, all of us can benefit from knowing, using, and understanding ways to develop and calm our limbic systems. All of us are impacted by emotions and relationships. Learning to understand emotions and relationships in terms of what is going on in our brain can be instrumental in helping to learn, grow, build relationships, and make decisions.

INTERVENTIONS

To learn what interventions can help to calm or develop the limbic system, let's think about young children again. The things that develop the limbic system are similar to the ways young children learn about their emotions and relationships.

The best way for children to learn about emotions is to feel them, talk about what they are feeling, and have a healthy, caring adult help them find ways to deal with that emotion. Putting words to emotions allows children to express them, understand them, and decide what to do about them.

To learn about relationships, young children need to experience healthy relationships. Once they have established healthy, safe, trusting relationships, they are free to explore new relationships with others. Usually this begins with one-on-one relationships with primary caregivers and then expands to relationships with siblings or peers. Group relationships are trickier and come after much practice with one-on-one relationships. Things inevitably go wrong in relationships. Children don't want to share, or may get rough with each other. Healthy adults model and teach children what is and isn't appropriate in relationships.

Bruce Perry speaks of core skills children need to be successful.[40] The first is attachment. Early attachment with healthy caregivers prepares children with the skills needed to regulate their impulses and emotions. Unhealthy attachment can spill over into other relationships and social skill development. Children who have problems with attachment usually struggle with regulation. If a child has poor regulation skills, they do not easily learn to get along with others because other children don't want to be around them. Without friendships, it is very difficult to learn empathy. Without empathy, there is little tolerance for differences. Without tolerance, respect for others is unlikely. All of these skills build on each other. They are developed as the brain develops from the bottom up.

Some children miss out on developing healthy attachment or learning good relational skills. This could be for many reasons. Some reasons might be:
* Parents or caretakers are not available or limited in available time
* Parents or caretakers model poor relationship skills
* Child struggles with regulation which keeps others at a distance
* Living environment is unsafe to practice relationship skills
* Early neglect or adversity interfere with attachment and ability to trust
* There is limited access to adults and/or same age peers

When unhealthy relationship styles have been developed, they can be changed. However, this will take a lot of repetition and work as new neural pathways need to be formed with positive caring adults and peers. Positive relationship skills can be learned through modeling, practice, feedback, and

> Learning to understand emotions and relationships in terms of what is going on in our brain can be instrumental in helping to learn, grow, build relationships, and make decisions.

repetition. Examples of activities or interventions that can help the limbic system are:

- One-on-one relationships with a safe, caring, attuned and attentive adult
- Counseling (individual or small group)
- Social skills training and practice with feedback
- Animal-assisted interventions (for some, due to past experiences, it may be easier to form attachment with animals)
- One-on-one friendships with healthy peers
- Team sports that involve individual participation (team participation may be too difficult depending on relational skills)
- Small group activities
- Community service
- Writing or journaling about emotions
- Spending time and talking with a safe, calm person when dysregulated (emotions are contagious)

Positive relationship skills can be learned through modeling, practice, feedback, and repetition.

Our need for relationships is as innately wired as our need to eat, drink, and sleep and is every bit as important. Positive, healthy relationships are important for our brain. We learn, grow, and regulate our actions better when we are around people who love and care about us.

ACTIVITY

What do you look for in a friend? Have students write down four qualities on four separate sheets of paper and then ball them up and throw them one at a time towards each corner of the room. Divide the class into four groups and send each group towards one corner of the room to retrieve the papers there. Have them read their papers and make a list of everything they have on a large sheet of paper that can be hung up in their corner. Then have each group share their list with the class. Discuss the similarities and differences between the lists. Share the following with your students:

If you have unhealthy relationship patterns, you can work to change them. Each new positive relationship potentially sets a new template for positive healthy relationships. Don't give up. Sometimes, people tend to move towards old relationship patterns with which they are comfortable. If you think this describes you, you can change this pattern. You can choose to pursue relationships that fit your list of positive qualities in a friend. Changing relationship patterns will take time. Your brain pulls you towards what is familiar and the unfamiliar can feel unsafe and scary. If you have struggled with relationships, here are things that might help:

- Practice your relationship skills with safe, caring adults.
- Keep your list of positive qualities in mind when looking for friends.
- Work to be the kind of friend that fits that list.
- Look for healthy, trustworthy people.

- Take small risks to know someone.
- Focus on the positive.
- You may want to talk with a counselor about past issues if you find yourself struggling with trust or attachment issues.

Reflection

MIRRORING EXERCISE

Have students break into pairs and stand face to face. One student leads the pair by making certain movements; the other student should mirror the same movement. Instruct the mirroring student to be very mindful of what the leading student is doing, including the emotions expressed and even their rate of breathing. Encourage the students to mirror as much as they can. After a few minutes, switch and have the other person lead.

Journal

Make sure each student has a journal and have art supplies available. Let students know journaling is their time to reflect and apply information learned in whatever way works for them. They can use words, colors, drawing or doodling.

9

Cortex

Cortex

Objectives & Materials

STUDENTS WILL BE ABLE TO:
- Review the processes the cortex controls
- Recognize signs of cortex dysregulation
- Determine activities that help develop the cortex

Materials:
- Visual items for four brain regions

Making Connections

Use a large dice to throw and have students answer the following review questions based on what number they roll. If they get the same number as someone else, they need to pick a different answer.
1. What is one intervention that can calm the brainstem?
2. What is one thing that the limbic system controls?
3. What is one thing that the brainstem controls?
4. What is one intervention that can develop the limbic system?
5. What is one intervention that can calm the midbrain?
6. Share an intervention that you have tried that is calming for you.

(Feel free to change these or add your own questions.)

Preparing the Brain

MINDFUL BREATHING COUNT
Introduce mindful breathing to your students:

You are always breathing and your breath is something that is always with you. Like an anchor, it can ground you to the present when your thoughts or emotions are taking you places you don't want to go. Taking deep, slow breaths can help calm you down when you are stressed.

Notice your breath right now. Where is it entering your body? Is it coming in through your mouth or nose? Does it leave your body through your mouth or nose? Continue to take deep, slow breaths. Where is the air going inside your body? Is your belly rising as you breathe in and gently falling as you breathe out? Continue focusing on your breath and count as you breathe. Say to yourself, "Breathe in one," "breathe out one," "breathe in two," "breathe out two." Continue to count your breaths until you get to ten.

Instruction The information in this chapter is based on the Neurosequential Model of Therapeutics (NMT) and the Neurosequential Model of Education (NME) developed by the ChildTrauma Academy. The brain diagram below is now filled in with all four parts. Today we will be focusing on the cortex.

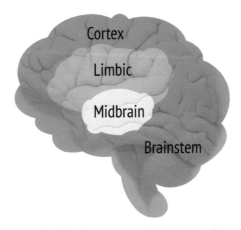

(Adapted with permission, © 2012 B.D. Perry)

Remember that the cortex is responsible for:
- Abstract thought
- Concrete thought
- Verbal and non-verbal communication
- Judgment
- Problem solving ability
- Insight/self-awareness
- Self-image
- Reading and writing
- Ability to modulate and control behavior
- Mathematical reasoning

Since the cortex is still developing through adulthood we all have the ability to continue to learn and get better in these areas. Every cortex is unique. It is possible for someone your age to be right on track for your age group with a cortical skill or to be developmentally years ahead or years behind, depending on the experiences you have had in life. This is why it is not helpful to compare yourself to others. If you are behind others your age in your reading ability, for instance, you are not "a bad reader," you just need more time and experience reading. Remember that neural connections are made by repetition. If you exercise your "reading muscle," it will grow. The same can be true for your communication skills, your ability to focus, your insight, your self-awareness, etc.

Some signs of an underdeveloped cortex will simply be skills that are lagging behind others your age in one of these areas. Remember that your cortex is the easiest part of your brain to change. If you want to improve your skills in any of these areas, you can. It is important to remember that you need to work in sequence from the bottom of the brain up. If there are underdeveloped areas in the lower levels of your brain, they will interfere with the improvements you want to make in your cortex. Some signs of an underdeveloped cortex may be:

- Inability to gauge time and time passing
- Difficulty interpreting non-verbal relational interactions
- Inability to regulate behavior/impulsiveness
- Communication problems
- Narcissistic or self-loathing behaviors
- Speech problems
- Poor insight and/or self-awareness
- Language or reading problems
- Difficulty thinking with numbers/mathematics

"In order to keep the brain fit, we must learn something new, rather than simply replaying already-mastered skills."[41]

NORMAN DOIDGE

Whether areas of your cortex are underdeveloped or not, all of us can benefit from strengthening the cortex. The cortex is responsible for your communication, decision making, and problem solving. You can always get better at these things. As you strengthen your cortex, you are strengthening your reasoning, impulse control, insight, creativity, and decision making. When the lower areas of your brain are well developed and regulated, you have the best access to this smartest part of your brain. Your cortex is what allows you to learn new things, think about what you are doing, make plans for the future, be creative, and solve difficult problems. A strong, healthy cortex is able to intervene and help you control your impulses and emotions. When your cortex, through self-talk and reasoning, helps you control the lower regions of your brain, this is called cortical regulation. You will be learning more about this in future lessons.

INTERVENTIONS

Anything that involves concrete or abstract learning, problem solving, creativity, insight, and/or communication strengthens the cortex. When you learn new skills, create art, converse with others, or explore new places, it strengthens your cortex. All of the things you are learning in school are strengthening your cortex.

Two important aspects of strengthening the cortex are repetition and novelty. If you practice the same thing over and over, that skill can get better and faster. When you try something new, your brain will actually form new neurons and new neural connections. Both of these are important for the growth and development of the cortex.

ACTIVITY

Have students list some things they think would be helpful in developing and strengthening the cortex. Have them list as many things as they can think of on the board. Use the following list to help prompt them or add to what they come up with.

Some examples of interventions that can help to develop the cortex are as follows:

- Reading
- Writing
- Mathematics
- Learning a language
- Puzzles
- Exploring
- Learning new things
- Sharing what you are learning with others
- Problem solving
- Insight-oriented counseling

Reflections

GRATITUDE MINDFULNESS ACTIVITY

Introduce the mindfulness activity:

It is easy at times to focus on the things that aren't going well or on the things we wish were different in our lives. What you focus on has a tremendous impact on your thinking, your emotions, and even your behavior. Today we are going to be purposely mindful of the things in your life for which you can be grateful.

Gratitude has powerful physiological effects on your brain and your body. When you think about things or people you truly appreciate, your body and brain become calmer. Research has shown that students who do daily exercises in gratitude, like keeping a gratitude journal, are more optimistic, feel better about school and life as a whole, and have fewer physical complaints.[42]

Make a list of things for which you are grateful. If you are struggling, consider something you have in your life from the list below, picture life without it for a brief second, and then take time to appreciate and be grateful for its presence in your life.

Here is a list to help students get started:

- Sunshine
- Home
- Clothes
- Electricity
- Indoor Plumbing
- Friendships
- Technology
- Clean water to drink
- Animals
- Nature
- Adults who care
- Ability to speak and understand
- Transportation
- Family
- Health
- Seasons
- Your five senses
- Food
- Entertainment

Journal

Make sure each student has a journal and have art supplies available. Let students know journaling is their time to reflect and apply information learned in whatever way works for them. They can use words, colors, drawing or doodling.

Responses to Threat

10

Responses to Threat

Objectives & Materials

STUDENTS WILL BE ABLE TO:
- Review the four regions of the brain
- Recognize the five states in the state-dependent functioning continuum
- Identify the area of the brain in control during each state
- Discuss the impact of state-dependent functioning on heart rate
- Compare and contrast the three different adaptive responses to threat

MATERIALS:
- Brain region visuals
- State-Dependent Functioning worksheet
- Picture/charade slips for each continuum state
- Optional: materials for collage
- Optional: video clips or pictures to demonstrate each continuum state
- Large dice

Making Connections

Hand each student a stack of papers with the words "brainstem," "midbrain," "limbic system," and "cortex" written on them. Each brain part should be on a different color of paper and each student should have three sheets of each color. Ask the following questions and have the student ball up the right color of paper and throw it towards the front of the room or aim for a trash can or container for each brain part. You will be able to tell how the students are doing by the color of paper they are throwing.
- This part of the brain controls my sleep and appetite (Answer: Midbrain)
- This is the smartest part of my brain (Answer: Cortex)
- This part of my brain controls large motor skills (Answer: Midbrain)
- This part of my brain is in control when I am in the state of fear (Answer: Midbrain)
- This is the part of my brain in control when I am calm (Answer: Cortex)
- This is the relational part of my brain (Answer: Limbic System)

- This part of my brain controls emotional reactivity
  (Answer: Limbic System)
- This part of my brain controls heart rate (Answer: Brainstem)
- This part of my brain is responsible for emotions
  (Answer: Limbic System)
- This part of the brain developed first (Answer: Brainstem)
- This part of the brain is the easiest to change (Answer: Cortex)
- This part of the brain develops in utero (Answer: Brainstem)

If you feel your class can handle it, after all the paper is thrown you can have students divide into two teams, gather up paper and then have a one-minute snowball/paper fight. This uses large muscle movement and some strategy and problem solving. After one minute, students are to pick up and count all the paper on their side of the room. The team with the least paper wins. This will get everyone active and laughing.

Afterwards, ask how each part of the brain was being activated during that exercise.
- Brainstem—increased heart rate and breathing
- Midbrain—large and small muscle movement
- Limbic—positive emotions, relationships, and teamwork
- Cortex—review and strategy in snowball fight

You may want to have students check pulse rates after the "snowball fight" to compare to pulse rate after the calming activity below.

Preparing the Brain

RELAXING BREATH
Walk your students through the following breathing exercise:

- Exhale completely through your mouth, making a whoosh sound to a count of six.
- Close your mouth and inhale quietly through your nose to a count of four.
- Hold your breath for a count of two.
- Exhale completely through your mouth again with a whoosh sound to a count of six.
- This is one breath. Now inhale again, and repeat the cycle three more times for a total of four breaths.

Note the six, four, two count. If you have trouble holding your breath, you can speed up, but keep the ratio at 6:4:2, always exhaling longer than you inhale. With practice you can increase the breaths. This relaxing breath is a useful tool to use when something upsets you, to calm yourself down.

Instruction

THE THREAT RESPONSE SYSTEM

This chapter is adapted from the Neurosequential Model of Therapeutics (NMT) and the Neurosequential Model of Education (NME) developed by the ChildTrauma Academy.[43]

Your brain is always on the lookout for threat and danger. It assesses information coming from both the external and internal world, and reacts instantaneously to assess the information and initiate the response that will keep you safe. A threat can be internal, such as hunger, lack of oxygen, or a stomachache. It can also be external, such as relationships, physical danger, a difficult academic challenge, or an emotionally uncomfortable situation.

Sometimes your brain's reaction to threat can be set off by something that is not an actual threat. A person may be in a safe environment and the brain can still respond as if the environment is dangerous. This reaction can be triggered by past experiences, and conscious or unconscious memories. A trigger can be a certain smell, a sound, a touch, a familiar face or anything that reminds you of the traumatic experience you have gone through before.

As you feel threatened, a complex, total body response begins which is directed and controlled by your brain. In order to help understand this complicated process, we will use a concept developed by Dr. Bruce Perry and the ChildTrauma Academy called state-dependent functioning. As your brain assesses that you are under threat, it shifts along a continuum of internal states to make sure you stay safe and have the resources you need to combat the threat. There are five internal states that function as a continuum. You can shift from one state to another in a split second or over a longer period of time as your brain's assessment of threat increases or decreases. The five internal states are:

- Calm
- Alert
- Alarm
- Fear
- Terror

At any given moment, you may be in a particular state based on your brain's perception of how safe an environment or particular situation may be. The brain, using memories and past experiences, makes a split-second decision as to which region of the brain needs to be more or less in control in order to best maintain your safety.

The following chart indicates which part of your brain is most in control during various states along this continuum. Essentially, the locus of control moves from the higher regions of your brain to the lower regions depending on the level of threat.

> **The brain, using memories and past experiences, makes a split-second decision as to which region of the brain needs to be more or less in control in order to best maintain your safety.**

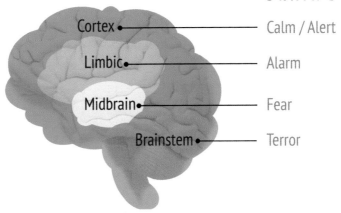

Cortex •———————— Calm / Alert

Limbic •———————— Alarm

Midbrain •———————— Fear

Brainstem •———————— Terror

(Adapted with permission, © 2012 B.D. Perry)

This is important because each region of your brain manages and processes information in a very different way. These internal states affect everything you do, including the way you think, act, and feel.

▶ INSTRUCTOR NOTE: Our students, especially the males, will often struggle with the states labeled "fear" or "terror." They vehemently deny that they are ever afraid. It is helpful to mention that often when under threat and moving through the continuum, the emotional reactions in the states labeled "fear" and "terror" are experienced as anger and rage.

HEART RATE

One physical thing that these internal states impact is your heart rate. The chart below shows how you will experience a physical change in heart rate based on what state you are in. It is important to note that heart rate ranges are approximate. Different people have different "normals" depending on a variety of factors. Basically, if your brain is preparing you to fight or flee from the threat, your heart rate goes up about ten beats per minute as you move down through these states as indicated by this chart. If your brain is preparing you to dissociate (zone out and shut down), your heart rate will go down as you move through this continuum towards terror.

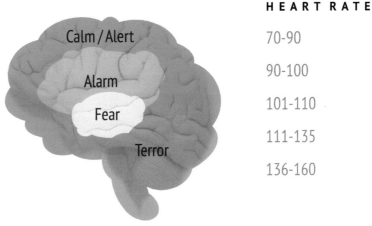

HEART RATE

Calm / Alert   70-90

Alarm   90-100

Fear   101-110

          111-135

Terror   136-160

(Adapted with permission, © 2012 B.D. Perry)

A normal resting heart rate for children ten years or older and adults falls in the range of 60-100 beats per minute. This would be lower for well-trained athletes and higher for younger children.

This information may be helpful in determining your state and allow you or the people who care about you assess the best course of action. If you feel yourself agitated and moving towards a state of alarm when there is no real danger and you are still able to access the thinking part of your cortex, you can use some of the exercises or techniques you have learned in this class to help calm yourself, lower your heart rate (or raise it if you are dissociating), and move back into an alert or calm state. If you have shifted to a brain state mediated by the lower brain areas, you may need others who care about you to help you return to a calmer brain state.

ADAPTIVE RESPONSES TO THREAT

Different people have different learned ways of responding as they feel threatened and move through this continuum of states. What feels threatening may be different for each individual, as well as which style of response they might use. There are two very different responses that people primarily follow when they feel threatened. Some people use a "fight or flight" response. Others use a "giving up or surrendering" response. Many use a combination of both these responses.

In the "fight or flight" response there is an increase in heart rate, blood pressure, body temperature, respiration, and muscle tone. You may feel your heart beating faster, your breathing rate increasing, and your temperature rising, and also notice that blood flow is increasing to your hands and feet. Your brain has sent signals to your body to be physically prepared to fight or run away from the potential threat. You may also find yourself hyper-focused on the threat while tuning out anything unrelated, so that you are no longer noticing or hearing extraneous things going on around you.

In the "giving up or surrendering," also called dissociative, response there is a decrease in heart rate, body temperature, and perception of anxiety and pain. Instead of becoming hyper-focused on the threat, you mentally withdraw from the outside world and focus on your inner world. You may tune out, feel detached or numb, stop responding to questions or directions from those around you, and lose your sense of how much time has passed.

Each of these responses can happen along a continuum. For instance, let's look at an example of the potential threat of an assignment that seems way too difficult for you. If you can stay in the alert state you can use your reasoning to find potential solutions, like asking for help from the teacher or working with a friend after class. If your brain assesses this as a significant enough threat and shifts to the alarm state, you may find yourself getting angry, arguing with the teacher, being disrespectful, being asked to leave the class, and storming out of the room kicking chairs and slamming doors on the way out. This would be an example of the "fight or flight" response. If you find yourself tuning out, putting your head down, completely shutting down and/or falling asleep, this would be an example of the dissociative response.

88

Those who use a mixed response might begin to shut down and zone out, but when pushed by the teacher shift into arguing and escalating to the point of storming out of the room. Others may begin by arguing, being disrespectful, verbally fighting with the teacher, and then at some point when they realize they can't win, shutting down and zoning out from the class and the teacher.

ACTIVITY OPTIONS
Brain State Pictures or Charades
Have small slips of paper with the states written on them. Have students take turns picking a slip of paper and then, without words or sounds, depicting that state for the rest of the class to guess. You can have them draw it or act it out. You could also allow them to choose which way to present it or use both mediums, depending on what makes them most comfortable.

Note that this is just practice to help in understanding the different states. We cannot always determine what state another person is in. People may seem calm on the exterior and really be in an alarm, fear, or even terror state.

Collage
Provide students with magazines and five sheets of paper or poster board. Have students designate a state to each poster board. You can simplify this into three posters by combining "Fear/Terror" into one and "Calm/Alert" into another. Have students cut out people, faces, or scenes from the magazines that they believe best represents each poster's state(s).

Video clips
Show video clips or pictures and allow students to discuss which threat response they think is being used.

Reflection

ACCORDION BREATHING
Introduce the following mindful breathing exercise:

> You have a built-in nerve whose purpose is to regulate and relax you. This is called the vagus nerve. This nerve travels down your spine and links your brain with your heart and gut. There is a simple ancient practice that activates the vagus nerve in order to relax the brain and body and protect you from stress. You can do this exercise sitting or standing.
>
> Bring your hands together in front of you with your palms touching. Notice the warmth between your palms and take a moment or two to focus on that. Now inhale and fill your belly with air as you move both arms outward like you are playing an accordion. When your arms are spread outward, hold your breath for a count of two. Then exhale

slowly while bringing your arms inward and your palms back together for a count of four. Let all of the air out and allow your stress to flow out with each breath. Repeat this five times.

Journal

Make sure each student has a journal and have art supplies available. Let students know journaling is their time to reflect and apply information learned in whatever way works for them. They can use words, colors, drawing or doodling.

State-Dependent Functioning

State-Dependent Functioning

Objectives & Materials

STUDENTS WILL BE ABLE TO:
- Discuss the impact of state-dependent functioning on thinking and decision making
- Recognize the impact each state has on thoughts, feelings, and behavior
- Discuss the implications that state-dependent functioning can have on long-term goals and planning
- Examine the benefits of understanding and recognizing state shifts in yourself and others

MATERIALS:
- *Antwone Fisher* DVD
- Visuals for each brain region
- Calming music
- Art or building supplies

Making Connections

In previous lessons, we looked at the concept of state-dependent functioning as a way to predict and understand how we are able to interact with our environment. List the five states and have students write what they remember about each. Have each state listed around the room on a large sheet of paper. Divide students into five groups. Start each group at a different state area. Have students work together to write everything they can remember about that state. Give a signal and have each group move to the next state and add to the list or place question marks next to anything they disagree with. Once the groups have arrived at the fifth state, have them stay there and present that state to the class. Have the brain visual or a picture of the visual for each brain region at the state area that uses that brain region.

Preparing the Brain

HOOK UPS WITH EIGHT COUNT BREATHS
Adapted from the *Brain Gym®* movement, Hook ups.
Walk the students through the following exercise:

While sitting up straight or standing, cross your legs, extend your arms out in front of you with your hands back to back and thumbs pointing down. Put one arm over the other and interlock your fingers. Then bend your elbows, bringing your interlocked fingers down and then up to your chest. Hold this position. As you inhale, place your tongue flat against the roof of your mouth, about one-quarter of an inch behind your front teeth. Relax your tongue as you exhale. Rest in this posture while breathing in for a count of eight and breathing out for a count of eight. Repeat this for six to eight complete breaths.[44]

Instruction

This chapter is adapted from the Neurosequential Model of Therapeutics (NMT) and the Neurosequential Model of Education (NME) developed by the ChildTrauma Academy.[45]

We learned in the last chapter that as your internal state shifts from calm to terror, the region of your brain that is in control changes. This is important because each region of your brain manages information, processes information, and solves problems in a very different way. These internal states affect everything you do. Understanding these states and their impact can be very helpful in understanding yourself and others. Today we will examine, in more detail, the impact of state-dependent functioning.

STATE-DEPENDENT THINKING

When you shift in the continuum of states and move from one region of the brain being in control to another, your style of thinking and decision making changes.

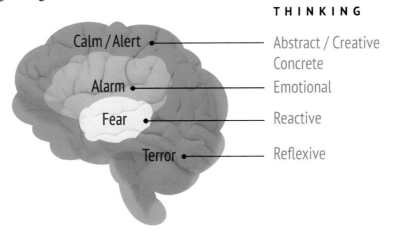

(Adapted with permission, © 2012 B.D. Perry)

When your brain is **calm**, you can think your best and be your most creative. You can think abstractly using the smartest part of your cortex and do your best problem solving. You are typically only in a calm state when you are alone in a quiet place and feel completely safe. This may happen when you are reading, writing in a journal, praying, meditating, or just relaxing. Imagine times when you have woken up with a brilliant idea or creatively solved a problem you have been struggling with while in a favorite quiet spot. This happens because you were in a calm state. As you move into your day, either at work or school, and are involved with people and facing new situations, you will shift into an alert state.

When you are in an **alert** state, you are in a great place for learning new things. You are using the lower, concrete thinking part of your cortex. You are still capable of solving problems, but your problem solving will be based more on experience and how you have solved similar problems in the past. In order to learn something new or be in a relationship, a small amount of stress is always present. This stress is positive. We need it to learn and grow. Our brains love novelty. This is the ideal state to be in at school or work, because you have the ability to take on new challenges and learn new things. To stay in the alert state, you still need to feel an overall sense of safety. If you begin to feel unsafe or encounter too much challenge, your brain will shift into the alarm state.

When you feel your safety being threatened, your brain shifts into the **alarm** state. In this state, your thinking becomes emotional as you are processing information through the limbic system. When in the alarm state, you are in tune with your emotions and the emotions around you. If in school, learning becomes difficult because you are more focused on the nonverbal and relational information around you rather than the content being taught. This state is uncomfortable and you will tend to react in ways to protect yourself. It is important to note that those who have suffered early adverse childhood experiences may find themselves in the alarm state even when no danger or threat is present. This state often becomes their baseline. They may need focused effort and help to move to a calm or alert state when in a safe environment.

When something happens to shift your brain into a state of **fear**, you are no longer thinking but basically reacting from the midbrain. This is helpful in a situation where you don't have time to think and need to immediately react. It won't, however, allow for complex problem solving as your problem solving will be completely reactive. If you find yourself in this state while in school, learning new information becomes impossible as you become hyper-focused on the perceived threat. Your main concern and focus is on what you need to do to deal with the situation and keep yourself safe. This is where your fight, flight, or dissociative response comes into play. This is a very uncomfortable state as you feel completely out of control. You may often find yourself, after the fact, forgetting what happened and/or wondering why you reacted the way you did.

If your brain shifts to a state of **terror**, your actions are completely reflexive coming from the brainstem. Your brain responds as if you are in imminent danger, and you have moved towards the extreme of your fight/flight or dissociative response. You are actively in the process of fighting, fleeing, surrendering, or shutting down. For those who dissociate, in the face of terror, they can even pass out.

As your brain moves into a fear, or terror state, you are functioning from a lower region of the brain and no longer able to think before you act.

> As your brain moves into a fear or terror state, you are functioning from a lower region of the brain and no longer able to think before you act.

STATE-DEPENDENT FUNCTIONING

Your thinking is either emotional, reactive, or reflexive, depending on which state you are in. If there is an actual threat to your safety, then your brain is in the perfect state. You need to be able to react quickly to real danger.

If, however, your brain shifts into alarm, fear, or terror when there is not truly a threat or dangerous situation, it is helpful to have an established safety plan. This plan should be thought through and practiced when you are in an alert or calm state. It should be shared with others who care about you and adults responsible for your safety. When you move into the alarm state and can no longer access your cortex, safe people can help remind and direct you to the plan you have established. If you have moved to a fear or terror state, it is helpful for others to understand how to help you feel safe and the importance of giving you the time, space, and interventions you need to return to a calmer state.

CHANGING FUNCTIONAL IQ

As your style of thinking changes so does your functional intelligence quotient (IQ). This is why the more alarmed, fearful, or terrorized you become, the less you are able to think clearly and logically. You actually become less intelligent. This is why if you become anxious while testing, you struggle to remember the answers that you knew before the test and will remember once the test is over. This is also why people often say things when they are angry or upset that they later regret, and why it is wise to never write an email, text, or post on social media when you are not in a calm or alert state. You become functionally less intelligent as you move through the states mediated by the lower brain regions.

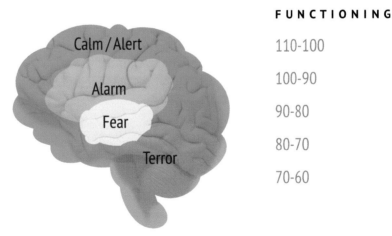

FUNCTIONING

State	Functioning
Calm / Alert	110-100
	100-90
Alarm	90-80
Fear	80-70
Terror	70-60

(Adapted with permission, © 2012 B.D. Perry)

Your state also impacts how you experience time. When functioning in a calm state, you can look far into the future, setting goals for the month, year, or even making a five- or ten-year plan. As you shift to the alert state, you are still able to plan ahead, but focus on what is happening in the next few days or week. When in the state of alarm, your focus is shifted to the next few hours or even minutes. In a fearful state, you care only about the next few minutes or seconds. If you find yourself in a state of terror, you lose all sense of time. This is why, after a bad accident, you may hear people say,

"It seemed like things were moving in slow motion," or after a near-death experience, people share that they saw their whole life flash before their eyes.

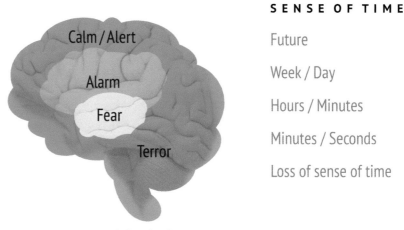

(Adapted with permission, © 2012 B.D. Perry)

This change in sense of time is important because when your brain shifts to a state mediated by the lower areas of your brain, you may find yourself reacting in ways that are not in tune with your actual values and goals. In the fear state, you are not thinking about graduation or the impact that your current behavior will have on your future, you are reacting to what feels like a threat to your current safety in the next few seconds or minutes. If you do experience a state-dependent shift like this, later, when you are in a calmer state and able to think more clearly, you may regret the long-term consequences of your actions or be puzzled over why you responded in that way.

DISCUSSION

Ask students to think of a time when they were in a state of alarm, alert or calm and their sense of time matched this chart. For example, when was the last time they thought about goals for the future? What state were they in? How about the last time they were in an argument with someone? How far ahead were they thinking?

CHANGING STATES ALONG THE CONTINUUM

Sometimes it seems pretty clear what state a person is in or when these states are changing. But sometimes people are able to look like they are in a calm or alert state when they are really highly agitated and reactive. Also, when people dissociate it can look a lot like being calm as the heart rate drops and they shut out the external world. It is important to remember that we can never truly know what state a person is in, but we may be able to pick up signs for those with whom we are close.

It is always wise to be sensitive and mindful about our interactions with others. What we see as joking, teasing, or having fun may be read by others as a threat to their safety. You may find someone reacts in a much stronger way than you had expected to something you did or said. If this happens, it is wise to stay calm, be understanding, and as much as possible, not react to their reaction. Like the analogy of the seltzer water, people may look calm on the surface when there is a lot of turmoil going on underneath.

Sometimes, it may be one significant or stressful event that leads us to a state mediated by lower brain regions, but at other times it may be an accumulation of frustrating and stressful situations that lead to a build-up and eventual explosion. As you have learned, what this looks like will be different for each person. For some, that reactive, alarmed state might mean yelling, cursing, or being disrespectful. For others, it might mean being passive aggressive, shutting down, or avoiding a friend or situation. It is important to remember that how you respond to people and situations is influenced by what state you are in. If you are having a bad day, you may react differently to a teacher redirecting you then you would if you were in a calmer state. Sometimes when in an alarm state, you may react in a disrespectful way towards someone and then later, once you've calmed down, regret how you responded.

It is very difficult to counteract a state-dependent shift in the moment. Once you move to the state of alarm, your cortex is not in control. You are no longer thinking concretely; you are responding emotionally. In this state, you are able to respond to safe and caring adults and friends as they direct you and try to calm you down. What can be helpful, especially if you move to the fear or terror state, is to make and share decisions and plans ahead of time regarding safe places you will go and things that help you calm down once you feel threatened. This is similar to practicing a fire drill before a fire occurs. If the drill was not known and practiced, there would be chaos in a school during an actual fire.

Your safety plan is like your fire drill. It needs to be practiced when you are not under threat, and shared with those who can help and direct you if you find yourself in a state of alarm, fear, or terror. Once the threat is gone, the physical interventions you have learned so far can be helpful in moving you into a calmer state. Also, if you practice these calming strategies consistently and learn what works for you, you'll be able to start your day in a calmer state and remain in that state longer throughout the day. Then, when normal challenges and frustrations occur, you may only be shifting to a heightened alert or low alarm state where you still have some access to your cortex and can make better decisions about how to solve the problem or calm yourself down. Understanding state-dependent functioning and practicing your safety plan can help you have better control in stressful situations.

ACTIVITY OPTIONS
Video Clip

Use a video clip from the movie *Antwone Fisher*. The beginning scene sets the background of Antwone's childhood history of prolonged abuse, which has impacted his interactions with his peers. Antwone Fisher grew up in foster care and experienced abuse as a young person. He signed up to go into the Navy, but his traumatic past was not resolved and it showed up as hair-trigger anger and ongoing conflict with his peers. The scene begins with a dream Antwone has had of a huge feast where he is surrounded by many people who love him. He has a huge stack of pancakes and can eat all he wants. In reality, Antwone's experience in foster care was one of abuse, disappointments, and heartache. Antwone wakes up, and he is now grown up and a sailor for the Navy. After the restless night of sleep, watch carefully what happens next as he interacts with other sailors on the ship. After you watch the clip, discuss the following questions:

- If you were another sailor on the ship would you have noticed something was wrong with Antwone?
- Do you think Antwone had an appropriate response to a sailor teasing him?
- Do you think Antwone was in real danger?
- What caused him to react the way he did?
- How does this clip relate to state-dependent functioning?

Visual Examples

Choose videos or pictures that represent people in different states along the continuum. Have students discuss what state they think the person/people are experiencing and why. See how similar the answers are. Discuss if there could be another possibility. Be sure to mention that it is not always possible to judge a person's state by what we see. Discuss the reasons why this may be the case.

Keep in mind that this is a continuum, there is certainly overlap in the behaviors that one will express when in each state. To simplify, especially for review activities, you may want to link calm/alert together, and link fear/terror together. Alarm can stand a little more easily on its own as the emotional/relational state.

Verbal Examples

What are some things that might cause someone to have a state-dependent shift and move from calm or alert to an alarm or fear state? Give a few examples and then have students list their own. The list below can be used to help if needed.

- You are cut off in the lunch line when you are already hungry and having a bad day.
- You are called on to answer a question in class and you don't know the answer.
- You find out your friends have been texting things about you that are untrue and hurtful.
- You leave for school after a huge argument with a parent or sibling.
- You realize that you have a test today you completely forgot to study for.
- You have studied for a test, and when you take it you forget all the answers and panic.
- You did not sleep well, woke up late, missed breakfast, and then missed the bus to school.
- You were yelled at in front of your peers by your boss at work for getting a customer's order wrong when you were trying your best and made a mistake.

Your safety plan is like your fire drill. It needs to be practiced when you are not under threat, and shared with those who can help and direct you if you find yourself in a state of alarm, fear, or terror.

- You tripped in the hallway in front of everyone and they are laughing at you.

ADDITIONAL EXAMPLE

If you feel the class would benefit from another example, you may choose to review the Zidane "head butt" incident from the 2008 World Cup. He was fouled hard, and in response, head-butted the other player. He was thrown out of the match and had extreme consequences afterwards.[46]

DISCUSSION

What are some possible clues that you are in a state of alarm or fear? This could include:
- Heart pounding
- Clenched fists
- Feeling nauseous in your stomach
- Sweating
- Yelling
- Unable to sit still (pacing)
- Putting head down
- Staring and not responding
- Feeling hot or cold
- Feeling hyper and agitated

What others can you think of? Why would it be important to recognize the clues that someone is in a state of alarm or fear?

Reflection

Play calming music for students. Allow them to use art supplies or some other substance (play dough, building tiles, etc.) to represent in colors symbols, and patterns, what it feels like to be in a state of calm.

Journal

Make sure each student has a journal and have art supplies available. Let students know journaling is their time to reflect and apply information learned in whatever way works for them. They can use words, colors, drawing or doodling.

Somatosensory Regulation

12

Somatosensory Regulation

Objectives & Materials

STUDENTS WILL BE ABLE TO:
- Recognize how information enters the brainstem through the senses
- Compare and contrast sensory experiences that calm and alert
- Understand regulation through sensory strategies (bottom-up regulation)
- Practice using their senses and movement to calm or alert the brain
- Determine what bottom-up regulation strategies are most helpful to them

MATERIALS:
- Calming and alerting activities (furniture, scents, drinks, food, chairs, music, exercise equipment)
- Magazines for collage
- Essential oils and cotton balls in storage bags
- Various sounds and music to play
- Fidgets

Making Connections

STATE-DEPENDENT FUNCTIONING REVIEW:

Have students break into groups of two or three. List the five states on the board. Instruct each group to come up with as many positives as they can about being in a calm or alert state. Then have them come up with as many negatives as they can about being in an alarm, fear, or terror state when no real danger is present.

After sharing lists, remind students that there are positives and negatives about each state. For instance, you want to be in fear or terror if you are being chased by a wild animal. That state will provide you the adrenaline you need to move fast. You don't want to be alert when you are trying to get to sleep, but it is a great state to be in when you are learning something new.

SWITCH CHANGE ROTATE ACTIVITY

Adapted from *101 Brain Breaks & Brain Based Educational Activities*.[47]

Divide students into groups of three to five. Have them line up single-file facing the front of the room. When you say "switch," the person in the front of the line moves to the back of the line. When you say "change," the person in front and the person in the back change places. When you say "rotate," everyone makes a 180 degree turn, now facing the back of the room. Repeat this multiple times. This is a great exercise to get the students thinking, focused, and working as a group.

After it is working well, change the instructions and say everyone in the line should call out one of the three words as quickly as possible. If two words are yelled out at the same time, the students need to decipher which one came first and follow all the instructions still but in the right order. Allow the exercise to go on like this for a few minutes. Hopefully it will be somewhat more difficult, disorganized, frustrating, etc. Keep a close eye on it and stop before it becomes too dysregulating for students. Share with the students how this activity has some similarities as to how state-dependent functioning works. Summarize the activity as follows:

> In this example, when I was clearly directing your decision making, you had to be thinking and staying in your cortex to decipher and follow concrete directions. When I was giving directions, the lines worked pretty well. When each of you could yell out a word, how did that feel? It got a little crazy, disorganized, inefficient, and/or frustrating. You were not at your best. Some of you began to respond more emotionally, lost track of where you were supposed to be, couldn't decipher the directions, even gave up. This frustrating few minutes can show you how what happens in your environment can cause a shift in your state. We are going to do a breathing exercise next to help you return to a calmer state.
>
> The problem in real life is that as you move out of the state of calm or alert, the cortex is no longer in control, and when it is not, your ability to listen, learn, and understand is impacted. A term that represents the cortex staying in control of the impulses coming from the lower regions of your brain is "cortical regulation." We will be looking at this and other types of regulation today.

Preparing the Brain

SQUARE BREATHING

Introduce the breathing activity:

> You have learned many different breathing exercises at this point. There are many other breathing exercises that you can find online, in phone apps or even make up yourself. The important thing is to be mindful

of your breathing, add rhythm to your breathing, and expand your breath deep in your lungs so that your belly rises. We are going to begin to repeat the exercises we have learned and see if you can comfortably add a bit more time to them. You can certainly bring in new options to share with the class and even lead the class in a breathing exercise in upcoming lessons if you would like. Today we will do square breathing from chapter 2.

Instruction

As we learned in the last two lessons, every brain is continually assessing how safe an environment or particular situation appears to be. The brain uses memories and past experiences to make a split-second decision.

When your senses tell your brain that something is wrong, the brain's alarm system will be activated, moving you into a state of alarm, fear, or terror. The heart rate increases, as well as the blood flow to the major muscle groups. Chemical reactions are activated that cause your body to prepare for a fight or flight response or a dissociative response to keep you safe from danger. You may become emotional, reactive, or reflexive. In these states your capacity to act in a thoughtful way using your cortex disappears.

The brain loves novelty, but with all novelty comes some degree of stress. Things like taking a test, completing an assignment, meeting new people, or developing a new skill all involve a bit of challenge, discomfort, and stress. The amount of stress caused by each situation will be different for each individual depending on their past experiences and their brain's assessment of threat. Remember that for those who have experienced early childhood adversity, the brain often develops an over-sensitive stress response system. These individuals may often find themselves in, or close to, a state of alarm. Taking on challenges will be extremely difficult if work is not done to move or keep the brain in a state of alert or calm. The strategies that help you move towards these calmer states are very helpful for all brains as they allow you to maintain control of your thoughts, emotions, and behaviors. If you catch yourself beginning to feel agitated, frustrated, anxious, or upset, it is helpful to have strategies that assist you in moving towards a calmer state. A term for this is "regulation." According to Perry, "regulation is the ability to put time and thought between a feeling and an action."[48]

We will be examining three different strategies for regulation, and each focuses on a different region of the brain. Top down or cortical regulation will use your cortex.

Relational and emotional regulation will use your limbic system. Bottom-up or somatosensory regulation will use your midbrain and/or brainstem. In this lesson we will be focusing on bottom-up or somatosensory regulation.

Somatosensory refers to the body and your senses. Your body and your senses send information directly to your brainstem and up through your midbrain. Using your senses and movement is a great way to stay

"Regulation gives us the ability to put time and thought between a feeling and an action."[48]

BRUCE D. PERRY

regulated and keep yourself in a calm or alert state. If a person has an overdeveloped stress response system and/or an underdeveloped cortex, bottom-up somatosensory strategies will be critical to controlling impulses and maintaining regulation. All regulation starts with the brainstem and midbrain. If they are dysregulated, you will have trouble accessing the higher levels of your brain to use relational or cortical regulation strategies.

You have already learned several interventions for the brainstem and midbrain using physical movement and your senses. Breathing exercises and mindfulness activities are examples of two of these interventions that you have been practicing regularly. Today we are going to explore, in more depth, the ability of your five senses and your movements to calm you down or wake you up as needed.

SENSES

All information enters the brainstem through one of your senses. Understanding your senses and sensory preferences is key to learning how to regulate your emotions, thoughts, and behaviors, and increase your ability to learn. A great resource regarding the impact of the senses on learning is *Take Five! Staying Alert at Home and School* by Williams and Shellenberger.[50] This book covers each of the senses thoroughly and includes many helpful activities.

ALERTING DISCUSSION

We can use our senses to calm ourselves down and to wake ourselves up. Ask students what things they do or see others doing to wake themselves up. Have students brainstorm things as you write them on the board. Note which sense(s) each item involves. Besides the five senses, students might put things on the list that pertain to the senses of movement, balance or unconscious awareness of body position. These are called the proprioceptive and vestibular senses. They are described later in the lesson.

- Eating (taste)
- Caffeine (taste)
- Candy (taste)
- Standing (large muscle and vestibular)
- Doodling (fine motor)
- Chewing gum (taste)
- Smell of coffee in morning (smell)
- Music with a strong beat (hearing)
- Talking with a friend (hearing, seeing, and limbic)
- Fidgeting with something (touch)
- Cell phone (touch, sight, and hearing)
- Exercise (large muscle, proprioceptive, and vestibular)
- Leaning back in a chair (large muscle and vestibular)

There may be some things on the list that don't apply directly to one sense. That is okay, just write everything down and try to get agreement regarding which senses are involved.

CALMING DISCUSSION

Ask students what things they do or see others doing to calm themselves down. Have students list these things and write them on the board. Have them discuss what senses these things relate to.

- Drinking calming tea (taste)
- Eating (taste)
- Calming smells and lotions (smell)
- Walking (large muscle, proprioceptive, and vestibular)
- Talking (hearing)
- Looking at something calming (sight)
- Nature (sight, smell, and hearing)
- Petting dog or other animal (touch, sight, smell, and hearing)
- Calming music—low beats per minute (hearing)
- Rocking (vestibular)
- Swinging (vestibular)
- Doodling (touch and fine motor movement)
- Exercise (large muscle, proprioceptive, and vestibular)
- Putting head down (vestibular)

Be prepared for answers regarding alcohol and drug use. Note that not all things on the list are healthy and we are looking for truthful answers as to what they have experienced or seen. Write it down along with everything else without much comment at the time, unless class reaction indicates a need for a comment. After the list is complete, acknowledge that there are healthy and unhealthy activities people use to activate their senses, which in turn influences the brain through the brainstem and midbrain.

Using your senses can send information to the lower levels of your brain to calm you or make you more alert. Some activities have more power than others and some activities will have a longer lasting impact than others. Let's look at each sense and think about its ability to calm you or make you more alert.

TASTE DISCUSSION

Encourage students to write down something that they can eat, drink, or chew on when they want to calm down, and also something they might use to wake up.

Your sense of taste can help you calm down or become more alert. Foods that have crunchy textures or cold temperatures are usually alerting. Also, for many people, foods that are spicy, sour or tart are alerting. Foods that are sweet or warm are usually good for calming. If they contain caffeine, however, they will most likely be alerting. Some foods can be helpful in either calming you down or waking you up. These are foods that require heavy chewing like hard pretzels or carrot sticks.

For some, chewing or sucking on nonfood items can be calming. Some people like to chew gum. Some chew on pens, pencils, toothpicks, coffee stirrers, fingernails, or suck on their hair or clothing.

Think about what you eat or drink when you are tired or want to wake up. Do you find yourself chewing on nonfood items?

TOUCH DISCUSSION

Your sense of touch can also help to calm you or to wake you up. Do you find yourself fidgeting with things? Do you tap your pencil, play with your hair, drum on your desk, or tap your feet? Maybe you love to curl up with a soft blanket. Fidgeting with items can calm anxiety and can also help to maintain focus and keep you alert. Pass fidgets around the room and invite students to experiment with them. Ask students what kind of textures they love or hate to touch.

A firm touch to the core of your body lasts longer than a light touch to your extremities. Pat yourself firmly on the back and notice the difference from the feel of that to the feel of lightly running your fingers up your arm. You may prefer one touch over another. Some people find the feel of a weighted blanket or lap pad calming. The feel of a soft blanket or material with a two-way stretch may have a similar effect.

Rhythmic tapping can be calming. Take a moment to tap your finger on your desk or on your leg. Notice how that feels. Does it feel differently depending on which hand you use? How about as you tap harder or lighter? Is there a difference between using your fingertips, fingernails, or whole hands? Note that tapping not only involves your sense of touch, but is also a rhythmic sound that impacts your sense of hearing.

In general, a cold environment or a light, unexpected or rough touch is often alerting. A warm environment or a predictable, patterned touch with some pressure is often calming.

Have students experiment with their sense of touch and list some of the ways they use it, or may be able to use it to keep themselves alert or calm themselves down.

VISUAL DISCUSSION

Sometimes there are things you can look at that can help you stay calm or return to calm. It may be a beach, ocean, beautiful flower, sunset, a favorite color, a cherished possession, a picture of a loved one, or a collage that exemplifies your goals. It may be a visual picture or, like you are learning from our mindfulness exercises, a picture in your imagination. What is something that for you, just seeing it, brings you a sense of peace or calm?

Do you like clutter or neatness? Bright colors or muted colors? Do you prefer few visual distractions or lots of things to look at? Do you prefer dim or bright lighting?

For the most part dim lighting, muted shades of blue and green, dark colors, and predictable rhythmic patterns can be calming. Bright lighting, shades of red and yellow, vibrant colors, and unexpected visual stimuli can be alerting. Electronic devices like smartphones, computers and TV's emit a blue light that signals our brains to stay awake. This is why it is wise to turn off electronic devices an hour or so before trying to get to sleep.

> For the most part dim lighting, muted shades of blue and green, dark colors, and predictable rhythmic patterns can be calming.

Have students choose pictures from a magazine that are calming or that bring them joy. Have them make a collage, or paste these pictures in their workbook or a small piece of poster board so that they can keep it with them and use it when they want to calm down or change their mood.

SMELL DISCUSSION

Certain smells can calm you down or wake you up. Provide some different scents for students to smell. Use essential oils and put a drop on a cotton ball that can be passed around in a container or plastic bag. Have students write down their reaction to each smell. Ask students: What do you like or dislike about the smell? Does it remind you of anything or bring up any picture or memory? What do you feel when smelling it? Is it calming? Disturbing? Energizing? Does it make you hungry?

In general, familiar smells that are associated with familiar comforting experiences, interactions or people are calming. Lavender, Pine, and Vanilla have been found to be calming for many people. Cinnamon, Citrus and Peppermint have been found to be energizing. All scents have the potential to trigger memories which could be calming, energizing or disturbing.

SOUND DISCUSSION

Ask students: What do you like to listen to? Do you prefer silence or music in the background when doing school work? What types of music wakes you up? What music calms you down?

In general, sounds that are most alerting are ones that are unexpected, of short duration, irregular and loud. A fire alarm would be an example of this. Sounds that are calming and easiest for the nervous system to ignore are ones that are familiar, quiet, patterned, rhythmic and repetitive. Music that has the same rhythm as a mother's heartbeat has been found to be most calming.

Play some sounds and/or pieces of music. Have the students record what they are feeling and thinking as they listen to each one. You can use things like the sound of an ice cream truck, television show theme music, calming music, energizing music, the sound of laughter, the music played in cartoons or movies when something bad is going to happen, etc.

MOVEMENT

Two senses that are connected to the body and movement are called the vestibular and proprioceptive senses.

▶ INSTRUCTOR'S NOTE: It is your choice whether to use these words or not. Feel free to simplify this for your audience if needed.

- **Vestibular**—The vestibular sense is our movement and balance sense. This sense is what keeps the body upright while standing, sitting, or walking. It "provides information about movement, gravity, and changing head positions."[51]

Slow rocking, linear motions, and repetitive, rhythmic movement have a calming effect on the nervous system. Usually, if you put your head down towards your chest it is calming and if you put your head back it is alerting. Have students try this and discuss the different feelings. Your head down mimics sleep and is usually the way your head rolls if you are falling asleep. When your head is back, it is a sensation similar to falling and usually will wake someone up.

- **Proprioceptive**—"Proprioception is the unconscious awareness of body position. It tells us about the position of body parts, their relation to each other, and their relation to other people and objects".[52] It gives us information from our muscles, joints, and bones and communicates how much force is necessary for muscles to exert. Even if a person is blindfolded, he or she knows through proprioception if an arm is above the head or hanging by the side of the body.

Certain types of proprioceptive sensations can help to regulate the midbrain. These sensations are provided by activities that require muscles to stretch and work hard such as wrestling, tug of war, pushing, pulling, carrying heavy objects, or chewing crunchy foods. An example of using this sense automatically when in a state of alarm would be when you tense your shoulders, arms and hands, or grasp the arm of the chair in a doctor's office while getting a shot.

In general, movements that are slow, controlled, patterned, and rhythmic can be calming, and movements that are fast paced, jerky, abrupt or change direction quickly can be alerting. For example, sitting in a rocking chair moving back and forth in a slow rhythmical manner will be calming to the nervous system. Rocking quickly in a jerky fashion will be alerting. When in doubt, stretching or using your large muscles in a controlled fashion is helpful in almost all situations. As mentioned earlier, this is one of the few things that can be effective to either calm you down or wake you up.

Reflection   FOCUSING ON SENSES

Introduce the mindfulness exercise:

> In order to give your brain time to reflect and put this information into long-term memory, we will do another mindfulness exercise. Hopefully you have become more aware today of healthy sensory experiences that you can use to stay calm and thereby improve your learning and control your emotions, behavior, and reactions. We are now going to do an exercise that will allow you to focus, and be mindful of the impact of your senses.
>
> Pay attention to your senses one at a time. First, focus on your sense of sight. Look around you. What do you see? Start with yourself. What do you notice about yourself, the position of your body, your clothes? Do

you notice what is in front of you? What is behind you? What is to your right or to your left? What do you see as you look around the room? Now move to your sense of smell. Do you smell anything? Notice the air move in and out through your nose. Take a moment to notice any scents that come with that air. Now move to your sense of hearing. What can you hear right now? What noises surround you? Close your eyes if you are comfortable and listen. Do you hear anything different with your eyes closed? Now pay attention to your sense of taste. What do you taste in your mouth right now? If you do not taste anything, what does "nothing" taste like? Finally, pay attention to your sense of touch. What can you feel right now touching your hands? What do your clothes feel like against your body? What is your body touching? If you are sitting, what is the feel of the chair? If standing, how does the ground feel against your feet? Continue to notice your senses for a few minutes, then open your eyes or look up when you are finished.

Journal

Make sure each student has a journal and have art supplies available. Let students know journaling is their time to reflect and apply information learned in whatever way works for them. They can use words, colors, drawing or doodling.

CHAPTER 13

Emotions and Sensations

13

Emotions and Sensations

Objectives
& Materials

STUDENTS WILL BE ABLE TO:
- Differentiate between sensations and emotions
- Identify sensations connected to their emotions
- Reflect on the varying intensities of emotions

MATERIALS:
- Visual items for brain regions
- Large sheets of paper to make life-size drawings
- Large dice
- Student workbooks or paper for activities
- Index cards

Making
Connections

In the previous lesson we learned about how your senses and movement can help to regulate or calm the brainstem and midbrain, and how they can also be used to help you stay alert and focused. Read a list of things involving the senses. If the thing is something that is known to be calming, have students put their head down on their desks. If it is something that is known to be alerting, have students stand up. If it does both, have students sit up straight in their chairs.

- Drinking coffee (A)
- Drinking warm milk (C)
- Eating something smooth and sweet (C)
- Eating something sour or tart (A)
- Eating hard pretzels (Both)
- Smelling lavender or lemon (C)
- Smelling peppermint or cinnamon (A)
- Dim lighting (C)
- Bright lighting (A)
- Slow rocking (C)
- Leaning your head back (A)

- Putting your head forward to your chest (C)
- Isometric exercises (Both)

Preparing the Brain

Allow students to choose a breathing break from the list of those you have taught them so far. You could list six to twelve breathing breaks on the board and have students throw one or two large dice to choose a brain break.

Instruction

SENSATIONS VS. EMOTIONS

The information in this chapter is adapted from the work of Diane Wagenhals.[53] Another great resource for additional ideas in this area is the work of Claire Murray.[54] As you remember from earlier lessons, all information comes into the brain by way of the brainstem through your senses. It can be very helpful to know the difference between sensory experiences (or sensations) and emotional ones. Sensations begin in lower brain regions and often precede emotional feelings. The degree to which a person can understand and manage painful or disorienting sensations may directly impact his or her ability to regulate emotions and behaviors. Recognizing sensations before emotional intensity increases can be instrumental in choosing regulation strategies before dysregulation occurs.

SENSATIONS

It can be helpful to recognize the wide variety of sensations you can experience. Sensations are different than emotions. They describe the physical way you feel in different areas of your body. They are not actions or behaviors, just physical feelings that occur in conjunction with an emotion. For example, if you feel like hitting something, the sensation might be tense muscles, clenched fists or a hot feeling in the neck and face, the action or behavior would be to hit something. A few examples of sensations would be butterflies in your stomach, a lump in your throat, or a racing heart. What are some sensations you can think of?

Have students brainstorm a list together. You may have to give students examples from below to get them started. These are sensations that you may feel in a particular place in your body:

- Butterflies in your stomach
- Flushed cheeks
- Headache
- Lump in your throat
- Dry mouth
- Racing heart
- Watery eyes
- Clenched teeth
- Tingly skin
- Blushing cheeks
- Tense shoulders
- Shortness of breath
- Nauseous stomach
- Weak knees

Other sensations might be felt in a specific place in your body or all throughout your body such as:

- Comfortable
- Pleasant
- Strong
- Weak
- Dizzy
- Achy
- Sweaty
- Hot

- Cold
- Burning
- Flushed
- Tight
- Sore
- Painful
- Tense
- Relaxed
- Restless
- Heavy

- Light
- Shaky
- Fidgety
- Wired
- Jittery
- Itchy
- Nauseous
- Numb
- Creeped out

It is important to be able to match your sensations with your emotions.

ACTIVITY

Hand out paper or have students do this activity in their workbooks. Students should independently write or draw on a picture of an outlined body, the sensations they feel with each of the listed emotions. Start with angry, sad, happy, afraid. If you have time, you can add surprised, disappointed, comfortable, confident, or other emotions.

Have students work in groups after they fill out their individual sheets. Give each group a large life-size piece of paper and an assigned emotion word. Have them trace one of their group members doing a pose for that emotion. Once they have a life-size outline of a body, they should fill in all the possible places and ways their assigned emotion can be felt. They can use words or drawings. When each group is finished, have them present and explain their drawing to the class. More sensations can be added by you and other class members as you discuss each drawing.

DISCUSSION

Have students share and compare the sensations connected with each emotion using either individual worksheets or the larger drawings. (If you didn't have groups do large drawings, you can have blank large drawings prepared ahead of time to fill in the different answers as students share.) Make sure to be prepared to add your own list of sensations that they may have missed.

EMOTIONS

When you describe an emotion, you are describing a mental reaction that is experienced as a strong feeling, arising spontaneously rather than through a conscious effort. Emotions can be responses to your experiences, relationships, thoughts, and even your own mood. They are a way to communicate how you are feeling in a given moment of time.

There is a difference between emotions and sensations, but they are often connected since you experience both in a relatively short amount of time. Every emotion activates a part of your body. Being aware of your sensations and their connection to your emotions can help you to be more mindful of an emotion before it gets too intense. When mindful of your emotions and sensations, you will be better able to take action before things get out of control. When you recognize the beginning stages of frustration, disappointment, anger, or fear, you can choose regulation strategies that can help you focus, calm down, and feel better.

The chart below shows emotions that are common, as well as times emotions can be more intense than at other times. It is important to understand that your emotions can be experienced on a continuum of high to low intensity. When mindful of your sensations as they connect to your emotions, you are better able to notice emotions before the intensity gets too uncomfortable. Recognizing emotions at lower intensity levels will allow you more time and more choices to regulate, focus, and feel better.

When you are mindful of your emotions, you can better control how you respond in a situation. Let's examine five emotions and see how they might look at varying intensities.

ACTIVITY

Have students break into five groups and give each group a set of index cards and an assigned emotion. Have them write different words for varying intensities of that emotion on the index cards and then put the cards in order from low to high intensity. (The order can vary from the order below. It is not important to agree on the exact order, just to recognize the differing intensities.) Have each group share their list and make a combined list on the board. You can use the list below to add other words as needed or to help groups that are struggling by giving some examples. You may need to give each group a high intensity and low intensity word from the list to get them started. For students that struggle with identifying emotions, you can write the emotions below on cards and have the students put them into categories in order of intensity.

Happy	Sad	Angry	Afraid	Comfortable
Ecstatic	Devastated	Outraged	Petrified	Peaceful
Thrilled	Depressed	Furious	Panicky	Confident
Overjoyed	Gloomy	Raging	Terrified	Relaxed
Delighted	Worried	Hostile	Frightened	Chilled
Excited	Rejected	Bitter	Intimidated	Appreciated
Happy	Discouraged	Mad	Threatened	Content
Cheerful	Unhappy	Frustrated	Afraid	Secure
Optimistic	Lonely	Aggravated	Scared	Safe
Pleased	Down	Annoyed	Anxious	Calm
Amused	Upset	Uptight	Nervous	Fine
Content	Disappointed	Upset	Tense	Okay
Satisfied	Moody	Offended	Wary	
Relieved	Let down	Grumpy	Cautious	
		Irritated	Uneasy	
		Impatient	Concerned	

Talk with the students about how different people can experience different emotions in the exact same situation. Being able to put words to your emotions and differentiate their intensity is an important skill to learn. Have students pick some emotion words from their list and give examples of when they might feel this way. (e.g. I feel grumpy when…; I am frustrated when…; I am furious when…)

"Emotional intelligence" is a term made popular by Daniel Goleman.[55] He defines this as "the ability to recognize, understand, and manage our own emotions, as well as the ability to recognize, understand, and influence the emotions of others." Developing emotional intelligence has been found to be a key to both personal and professional success.

Learning to recognize your sensations and identify your emotions can help you determine when regulation strategies are needed. This understanding is an important step on the path to emotional intelligence.

Reflection

EMOTIONS AND SENSATIONS
Introduce the mindfulness exercise:

Sit quietly and take some deep breaths. Scan your body for sensations from the list we discussed today. What sensations are you feeling? Don't judge them, just notice them. If you feel tension, try to let it go with each breath you take. Notice any emotions that are present as you breathe. Again, don't judge them, just notice them and name them. Continue to breathe deeply. If there is an emotion you don't want to hang onto, imagine sending it out of your body bit by bit with each breath. Continue relaxing and breathing in calmness with each breath and exhaling any sensations, emotions, or thoughts you do not want.

Journal

Make sure each student has a journal and have art supplies available. Let students know journaling is their time to reflect and apply information learned in whatever way works for them. They can use words, colors, drawing or doodling.

CHAPTER 14

Relational Regulation

14

Relational Regulation

Objectives & Materials

STUDENTS WILL BE ABLE TO:
* Discuss relational regulation strategies
* Experience the impact of mirror neurons
* Compare and contrast relational regulation with relational dysregulation

MATERIALS:
* Visual items for brain regions
* A paragraph, short story, or children's book about friendship
* Instructions for role play

Making Connections

PARTNER OR TEAM REVIEW

Since today's lesson is about relational regulation, we will review in pairs or small groups. Decide what size groups will work best for your students. Have the following statements or questions written. Assign one to each group. Have each group discuss and come up with the answer to their assignment and share their answers with the class.

* Describe the difference between emotions and sensations
* List sensations you might experience when you are in the state of alarm
* List sensations you might experience when you are in the state of calm
* List words that identify varying intensities of happy
* List words that identify varying intensities of angry
* List words that identify varying intensities of fear
* List words that identify varying intensities of sadness

Preparing the Brain

Allow students to choose a calming brain break from those you have done so far. It is fine if they each pick their own and do it individually. Set a timer and have students all start and finish at the same time.

Instruction

The information in this chapter is adapted from the Neurosequential Model of Therapeutics (NMT) and the Neurosequential Model of Education (NME) developed by the ChildTrauma Academy.

You have learned that the bottom two levels of your brain can be regulated by physical interventions involving your senses and movement. You have also discovered that your sensations are connected to your emotions, and that these emotions have varying degrees of intensity. Your sensations are controlled by the lower regions of your brain and can be impacted by the brainstem and midbrain interventions we have discussed. Your emotional reactivity is controlled by your limbic system, which is also responsible for your relationships.

As you become uncomfortable in a situation and move towards a state of alarm, your limbic system begins to take control. If you are able to identify sensations and emotions while you can still access your cortex, you will be able to make decisions and choose regulation strategies to help keep you regulated. Once your limbic system takes over, your cortex is no longer in control and your thinking and decision making becomes emotional. You are tuned in to and impacted by the emotions and nonverbal signals of those around you. If those around you are calm, safe, and caring, they may be able to help you push through the uncomfortable feelings and return to a calmer state. This is relational or limbic regulation.

For example, imagine you are worried about a test coming up. You have studied and felt prepared, but as you enter the classroom your anxiety level rises and you can't remember much of what you learned. A friend who you have studied with encourages you to take a number of deep breaths as she recognizes that your anxiety level is rising. She reminds you calmly that you studied, and that you know the information. She believes in you and tells you that you've got this. In this scenario you would most likely begin to calm down and regain access to the information stored in your cortex. Your friend's level of calm was contagious, along with her belief in, and affirmation of, your ability. The limbic system is best regulated by the presence of safe, caring, positive relationships.

The opposite would happen if your friend was just as anxious, or even more anxious than you. Imagine if your friend was losing it and saying things like, "What if we studied wrong? We can't fail this test! If we fail this class we won't graduate! Oh no, I can't remember a thing!" This friend, although possibly very caring and committed to your friendship, would not be a help to you in regulating your limbic system. You would both become quite dysregulated. Hopefully, a caring teacher would notice and encourage both of you to take some deep breaths. Then with the teacher's encouragement and contagious sense of calm, you would both calm down, and regain access to your cortex.

ACTIVITY

Choose two students who have both leadership and acting skills. Have them leave the room and then come back and read a short story about friendship. This could be *The Giving Tree* by Shel Silverstein[56] or any other children's book, article, or short story. The first student should read the first half while yawning and acting a bit bored. Then the second student should read the second half with emotion, and smile when appropriate, especially when happiness is mentioned. Encourage the two students to make it somewhat natural, not "over the top" obvious. During the reading, note how many times other students yawn during the first presentation and smile during the second. The student who knows what is happening, but is not the one reading the story at the time, can help you note the number of yawns or smiles.

Afterwards, share with the students what was going on and discuss what they felt during each reading. Share how emotions can be contagious because of mirror neurons. Point out that if the expressions of the person reading the book impacted you, it is a good example of your mirror neurons at work.

MIRROR NEURONS

Mirror neurons are a special class of brain cells that fire not only when you perform an action, but also when you observe someone else performing the action. These neurons allow you to not only understand another person's actions, but to feel what they are feeling. For example, when you see someone smile, your mirror neurons for smiling fire up too, creating a sensation in your own mind of the need to smile. When you see someone yawn, you feel the need to yawn too. This is why it is so crucial that you choose your relationships carefully. Emotions are contagious. If you are around negative people who are complaining about a lot of things, you will begin to feel negative. When you are around positive people who are seeing the best in a situation, you will feel more positive. You are impacted by those you associate with. You also have the ability to impact others.

DISCUSSION

Ask students what they think the previous quotation means. What are some of the positives and negatives about fire? About water? About wind? How does this relate to relationships?

RELATIONAL OR LIMBIC REGULATION

Your relationship templates or patterns were established during your early years of life. As a baby, your brain made connections regarding people and what to expect from them based on those who first took care of you. If your needs were met, your brain decided that people were to be trusted. If your needs went unmet, or those who were supposed to care for you hurt you, your brain decided people were not to be trusted. If those caring for you were inconsistent, your brain decided that people were unpredictable. Whatever patterns were established became deeply ingrained as your brain formed its first neural connections and pathways regarding these first relationships in life.

As time went on, you experienced many other relationships, both good and bad. With each new relationship and interaction, your brain had to decide whether the new relationship fit with the strong neural pathway

"Fire can warm or consume, water can quench or drown, wind can caress or cut. And so it is with human relationships: we can both create and destroy, nurture and terrorize, traumatize and heal each other."[57]

BRUCE D. PERRY

already formed, or whether it was different and needed a new neural pathway. It is easier to place people on an already existing pathway than to form a new pathway. It takes more effort and repetition to form new pathways. Those who learned early not to trust may push people away assuming they can't be trusted, even when they are very safe and caring. If these people persist and don't give up, in time, a new neural pathway will be formed for them, representing a caring person pathway which others can be placed on later as well.

As an example, imagine you have experienced many struggles with teachers through the years. You have not felt respected, cared for, or safe. Your first reaction and expectation with any new teacher will be that they are like all the rest and won't respect or care about you. When a new teacher shows a genuine interest in you, you may assume it is a trick, and respond rudely or shut down. Your brain puts them on the strong neural pathway for teachers already formed, and you refuse to give them a chance. If they persist and don't give up on you, over time and after many repeated attempts at genuine caring, your brain decides that this situation is different and forms a new neural connection and pathway for a teacher that cares. The same thing can happen with friendships and other types of relationships.

It is important to have people in your life who care about and support you. You will do your best learning and decision making when you feel cared for and safe. Positive relationships can help regulate you and keep you safe. You can take more risks at learning new information, developing new skills, and changing behaviors when you are in the presence of those who care about and support you. If you are feeling anxious or upset, the presence of a calm, safe, caring person will help regulate you and move you back towards calm. For this reason, some students feel most comfortable and in control when their desk is close to the teacher's desk or to that of a best friend.

Sometimes your relationships can cause an escalation in your emotional reactivity rather than helping you calm down. This is important to consider when choosing a person to talk to about a problem, and when being that person for someone else. We all need people to talk to when we are upset. Often, however, we are drawn to those who agree with us and will tell us how right we are to be upset. They might get upset as well, even possibly more upset than us, fueling the fire of our emotions and causing our anger to escalate. Together, we move into a state of alarm where we are not thinking, but reacting emotionally and encouraging each other to respond in ways we may later regret.

A better scenario would be to talk with a friend or adult who is able to stay in a calmer state and talk rationally, rather than emotionally, about what is upsetting you. Since emotions are contagious, a calm friend or adult can help your emotions decrease in intensity and allow you to move towards a state of calm. This is relational regulation. Having people in your life who can be trusted to help you return to a calmer state by staying calm themselves is very important. When you are upset and move to a state where your cortex is no longer in control, it is helpful to have someone else who can function as your cortex temporarily by staying calm and giving you the clear direction you need to return to a calmer state. Hopefully, you are able to be this person for others at times by remaining calm and not feeding the fire of their emotions when they are upset.

Relationships are complicated. You may have people in your life who are always supportive and able to keep you calm, but there are probably many other relationships that are at times helpful, and at other times unhelpful. All of us can move into the state of alarm without notice and become emotionally reactive. This can happen in the middle of a conversation which was, up until that point, positive and helpful. It is important to be aware of our impact on each other. When a conversation becomes one that is fueled by emotional reactivity for both people involved, it is wise to take a break from that conversation and find another way to calm down.

ROLE PLAY ACTIVITY

Have one student share a stressful situation with a partner. Make sure it is an imaginary or safe one to share in front of the group. You can write a problem out yourself or use the suggested examples below. This can be done with the whole class broken into groups of two or three with one person being assigned to observe. You could also choose one courageous person to do it in the front of the room for the rest of the class to observe, with another student or you being the listener.

Give the listening partner a slip of paper with two sets of role play instructions to apply to the example situation. The first time they should get anxious or upset with the situation, stating things like, "I can't believe that happened! You should be really nervous/angry/afraid" (whatever the emotion being expressed is, but escalated). They should urge on the person in any negative emotion expressed, telling them how awful it is and how they have to do something about it, encouraging reactive rather than thoughtful responses. After a couple of minutes, stop the role play. Be careful not to let it go on too long as it can be quite uncomfortable and cause dysregulation for both the students participating and others observing. Ask the person sharing the role play situation how this felt. Ask the listener and anyone observing what it was like for them.

Then, have the same person share the exact same situation again. This time, instruct the listener to stay very calm, listen attentively, and give short, positive affirmations about how capable the person is to handle this situation. Model good, deep breathing skills as you listen. After a few minutes, ask how it felt. Did it feel different? What did people notice? Hopefully you will have a good discussion about the difference between regulating and dysregulating conversations.

SUGGESTED ROLE PLAYS:
- You are struggling to understand Algebra. The teacher goes too fast for you and seems to get frustrated when you ask a question. Most of the time you don't even know what question to ask. You are so lost! If you fail this class, you will not be able to graduate on time.

- Your best friend is having a party and didn't invite you. He or she says that your invitation must have been lost but you know that is not true. There is a new group that he or she has been hanging out with and you feel as though this group does not accept you. You are worried that you might be losing your best friend and frustrated that he or she may be lying to you.
- There is a new student in school that seems to have it out for you. He is always bumping into you in the hallway. He has made disrespectful comments under his breath and is starting to say things out loud whenever you walk by. You don't know what his problem is but find yourself getting angrier and angrier. You don't want to get into a verbal or a physical fight, but you are worried that that is where this is heading.

Reflection

MINDFUL MIRRORING EXERCISE

Have students break into pairs. One student leads the pair by making certain movements and expressions and the other student is to mirror the same movement and expression. The mirroring student should be very mindful of what the leading student is doing, including the emotions expressed and even the rate of breathing. Have the leader, without sound, express some strong, nonverbal emotions through facial expressions and body language. Start with negative emotions like anger, disappointment, frustration, fear, or boredom. Have them roll their eyes, shake their head, yawn, etc. Then move to positive emotions like happiness, contentment, joy, or peace. Have students mirror as much as they can. After a few minutes, switch and have the other person lead. Ask both people to be mindful of how they are feeling when mirroring the emotions of another. Afterwards, discuss the impact. Did they feel some of the emotions they were mirroring? Do they think their mirror neurons were activated?

Journal

Make sure each student has a journal and have art supplies available. Let students know journaling is their time to reflect and apply information learned in whatever way works for them. They can use words, colors, drawing or doodling.

CHAPTER 15

Cortical Regulation

Cortical Regulation

Objectives & Materials

STUDENTS WILL BE ABLE TO:
- Review relational regulation strategies
- Discuss cortical regulation strategies
- Practice cortical regulation strategies

MATERIALS:
- A soft ball
- Colored paper for gratitude chains
- Pictures for empathy exercise
- Student workbooks or a self-talk worksheet

Making Connections

WOO WAH WISH ACTIVITY

This activity is adapted from *101 Brain Breaks & Educational Activities*[58]

Have all the students sit in a circle. Using a soft ball, throw the ball to each other. If you throw the ball to the person directly to your right you have to say "woo." If you throw the ball to the person to your left you have to say "wah." If you throw the ball to anyone else you say "wish." You cannot have two of the same kind of throws in a row, so if the person who threw you the ball said "wish," you have to either do a "woo" or a "wah." After a little while if this seems to be going well, change the tone of voice you are using, saying the same words but now screaming them with a sense of either anger or fear. Don't do this for too long as it will be quite dysregulating. After a couple of minutes, stop and discuss the activity.

In this activity, you very much need access to your cortex to remember the difference between woo, wah, and wish and to keep track of throwing, catching, and doing something different than the person before you. It was hard already because of the stress of keeping up with all the rules. You may have become too stressed and struggled to maintain access to your cortex to make the needed decisions. When the instructions were changed to screaming the words, you likely struggled even more with maintaining the directions. This is an example of your brains moving to the state of alert with the limbic system being in control. When voices were raised with emotion, the emotions became contagious and you were triggered to interpret the loud voices as a sign of threat.

Preparing the Brain

Make sure to do a nice long breathing break to allow students to calm down after this activity. You can choose one or allow students to choose from the list of those you have done so far. It is fine if they each pick their own and do it individually. Set a timer and have students all start and finish at the same time.

Instruction

CORTICAL REGULATION

The third type of regulation we will talk about is cortical regulation. When the other areas of your brain are regulated, you have the best access to this smartest part of your brain, your cortex. Your cortex is what allows you to learn, think, be creative, and solve problems. A strong, healthy cortex is able to intervene and help you control your impulses through reasoning and problem solving. When your cortex is able to help you control the lower regions of your brain, this is called cortical regulation. This happens for most people on a regular basis when they are in a state of calm or alert. When your cortex is in control, you are able to do your best thinking and problem solving. You can even examine your thoughts and change them as needed to help you respond to the situation.

Cortical regulation involves using the cognitive skills of reasoning, critical thinking, self-monitoring, problem solving, planning, and insight. When the bottom levels of your brain are regulated, you can use these cognitive abilities to:

- Modify or challenge your unhealthy thoughts
- Plan and organize
- Problem solve healthy options for getting your needs met
- Set goals and reinforce healthy behaviors
- Practice empathy
- Practice gratitude
- Participate in counseling

With your cortex in control, you are able to think clearly and have access to all your problem-solving abilities. If you are lacking in knowledge regarding a particular problem, you can gather the information and knowledge you need to make the best possible choices.

You are able to converse with positive, healthy people in your life to get perspective on your thoughts and patterns. If your thoughts and self-talk are negative, you can change them and rethink your approach to a problem.

Counseling with a professional can also be a big help if you find yourself stuck in unhealthy behaviors or thought patterns.

We are going to practice some activities today that are examples of ways your cortex can help change your thoughts, regulate your emotions, and impact your behaviors.

PRACTICING GRATITUDE

Gratitude is a way of thinking that allows you to change your focus. It has been shown to have a significant impact on a person's health and wellbeing. When you are able to access your cortex, you can choose to focus on what is good and positive in your life, and be thankful for it rather than choosing to focus on the negative. Your choice of focus will impact your attitude, emotions, and wellbeing. That is why, through the process of journaling, we have been asking you in each class to write something you are thankful for. Hopefully this is helping to form a habit for you and a strong neural pathway for gratitude.

ACTIVITY

Have students list five things they are grateful for and write them on five different strips of paper. Connect these strips into rings to form a chain and hang this gratitude chain around the room to remind students to focus on the positive things in their lives.

PRACTICING EMPATHY

Every individual is unique. No one like you ever was and no one like you will ever be again. Besides the differences in personality, strengths, weaknesses, backgrounds, and culture, there is a unique wiring of your brain caused by unique experiences, forming unique connections and memories. For this reason, two people can see the same event or have a conversation and come away with surprisingly different accounts.

For example, eye witness accounts tend to be inaccurate. Five people interviewed after a robbery may give completely different accounts of the suspected robber's height, weight, hair color, and ethnicity.

Your cortex has the ability to enable you to put yourself mentally in another person's place and try to understand what they are feeling and/or experiencing. This is something that is learned over time as you relate to others, ask questions, and attempt to understand differing perspectives. Your ability to empathize will increase with practice and experience as you allow yourself to listen to different perspectives and relate to others who are different from you.

ACTIVITY

Have students view various pictures and record the first thought that comes to their minds. Choose pictures that will get mixed reactions such as: a spider, a half-filled glass, optical illusions, people sky diving, or people arguing. Have students record answers to the following questions:

"Reflect upon your present blessings, of which every man has plenty; not on your past misfortunes, of which all men have some."[59]

CHARLES DICKENS

- What do you see?
- How does it make you feel?
- Does it remind you of anything?
- What do you think these people are doing or feeling?

Have students share their responses and compare and contrast responses with others in the classroom. Ask how their perspectives are similar or different than that of their classmates. Explain how individuals develop varying perspectives based on experiences and connections their brains have made. Because we all view things differently, it is important to take time to understand the perspective of others before drawing conclusions.

SELF-TALK/AFFIRMATION

The things you say to yourself are very important. Your self-talk impacts your thoughts, emotions, and your regulation. If you are in a difficult situation and you say to yourself, "This is out of control, I can't handle it. I never do well in these situations, so why even try?", these thoughts will impact your emotions and your behavior. If, on the other hand, you say to yourself, "It's ok. Things may be tough right now but I am tougher. I've been through worse, and I can handle this!", you will have a completely different emotional reaction and response. You can control the things you say to yourself. Even if you don't believe the words at first, saying positive things over and over will impact your thoughts, emotions, and behaviors.

Try this: write down something you would say to yourself when faced with a difficult challenge. Is it positive or negative? If negative, rewrite it and say it to yourself. How does this feel? Even if you don't believe the positive affirmation yet, say it over and over throughout the week as much as possible. You will notice a change over time.

ACTIVITY

Use the situations and statements below and have students change the negative statements into more positive statements. You could also have students write their own or do a combination of both.

Change each statement into a positive response to the same situation. The first two are done for you.

- You fail a test.
  Negative statement to self: I am stupid.
  Changed statement: I didn't do well on this test, but I can learn this information. If I take more time to study, I will do better next time.
- You trip and drop your books in the hallway.
  Negative statement: I am such a klutz.
  Changed statement: Everyone falls sometimes; it is not a big deal.
- Your boyfriend or girlfriend breaks up with you.

Negative statement: I am such a loser; no one will ever love me.
Changed statement:

- You get anxious and can't remember the information you studied for a test.
Negative statement: Why bother studying? My brain never works the way it should.
Changed statement:

- You have a fight with a friend and you both say mean things that you truly regret.
Negative statement: Why do I pick such horrible friends? No one really cares about me.
Changed statement:

- A teacher has to redirect you for talking too much in class.
Negative statement: This teacher hates me. Why bother trying to please her?
Changed statement:

- You feel depressed.
Negative statement: Something is wrong with me. I am never going to be happy.
Changed statement:

- You try out for the basketball team but don't make it.
Negative statement: I am just not good enough to play sports. I give up.
Changed statement:

- You are irritated by comments classmates are making.
Negative statement: I can't handle these people. I'm walking out of class or hitting someone.
Changed statement:

- You are unhappy with your appearance.
Negative statement: I am too ugly, fat, skinny, tall, short (whatever you might feel).
Changed statement:

Reflection MINDFUL THOUGHTS

Introduce the mindfulness exercise:

Take a deep breath and relax. Notice your thoughts as they move through your brain. Just because you think something doesn't make it true or real. Thoughts can come and go. Some thoughts stick with you for a while, others come and go quickly. Notice some of the thoughts you are having right now. Stop and consider them for a moment. Are they positive or negative? Maybe they are judgments? A judgment is just an opinion. Don't focus on judgments. Take a moment to recognize it, but then return your attention to your breathing and let it pass. If you are not having any thoughts that come to focus, that is fine.

Continue to relax and breathe slowly, just noticing what is happening without judgment. There is no right or wrong way to be mindful. If you find thoughts entering your mind that cause uncomfortable feelings of fear, anger, or anxiety, notice them but bring your focus back to the present and to your breathing. You can stop this exercise any time if it is uncomfortable. If you are okay with your thoughts, continue to take deep breaths and notice where your mind goes.

Journal

Make sure each student has a journal and have art supplies available. Let students know journaling is their time to reflect and apply information learned in whatever way works for them. They can use words, colors, drawing or doodling.

CHAPTER 16

Regulate, Relate, Reason

16

Regulate, Relate, Reason

Objectives & Materials

STUDENTS WILL BE ABLE TO:
- Recognize the need for regulation to remain in a calm or alert state
- Understand the sequence of engagement: Regulate, Relate, Reason
- Recognize possible triggers for shifting to states of alarm or fear
- Compare and contrast regulation strategies for different regions of the brain
- Refine personal safety plan
- List the regulation strategies most helpful to them

Making Connections

MATERIALS:
- Stacks of paper with a brain region written on each page
- Regulate, relate, reason worksheet
- Brain region visuals

Divide the students into two teams, with one team on each side of the room. Draw an imaginary line down the middle of the room and have them turn their desks to face each other. Hand each student on one side of the room two stacks of papers with one brain region listed on each: Brainstem and Cortex. Hand each student on the other side of the room two stacks of papers with one brain region listed on each: Midbrain and Limbic System. Each student should have at least six total pieces of paper, three of each word.

Instruct the class that when you make a statement, if the answer is one of the brain regions they have in front of them, they are to ball up a piece of paper with that brain region on it and throw it to the other side of the room. If you want, you can give them more paper to start and allow them to throw as many as they can until you stop and move on to the next statement. You should be able to tell how the students are doing by the side of the room throwing paper. Make sure to state the right answer before moving on in case some might have just thrown a paper because they saw their teammates throwing paper. This will help to reinforce the correct answer for everyone.

- This part of my brain does not think, but reacts (Answer: Midbrain)
- This is the smartest part of my brain (Answer: Cortex)
- This part of my brain controls large motor skills (Answer: Midbrain)
- This part of my brain is in control when I am in the state of fear (Answer: Midbrain)
- This is the part of my brain in control when I am calm (Answer: Cortex)
- This is the part of my brain in control when I am in the alarm state (Answer: Limbic System)
- This part of my brain controls emotional reactivity (Answer: Limbic System)
- This part of my brain controls heart rate (Answer: Brainstem)
- This part of my brain is responsible for emotions (Answer: Limbic System)
- This part of my brain developed in utero (Answer: Brainstem)
- This part of my brain is the easiest to change (Answer: Cortex)
- This part of my brain is in control when I am in a state of terror (Answer: Brainstem)

If you feel like your class can handle it, after all the paper is thrown you can have students gather up paper and then have a one-minute snowball/paper fight. This uses large muscle movement and some strategy and problem solving. After one minute, students should pick up and count all the paper on their side of the room. The team with the least paper wins. This will get everyone active and laughing.

Afterwards, ask how each part of the brain was being activated during that exercise.
- Brainstem: increased heart rate and breathing
- Midbrain: large and small muscle movement
- Limbic: positive emotions, relationships, teamwork
- Cortex: review and strategy in snowball fight

You may want to have students check pulse rates after the "snowball fight" to compare to their pulse rates after the calming activity below.

Preparing the Brain

It will be important to take the time to calm students down through a breathing break of significant length. Belly breathing from chapter 3 is a good break to use. Remember to have students record their heart rate before and after to see what impact both exercises have had on their heart rate and brainstem. You can begin teaching while they are still in a relaxed position with their hands behind their head. Encourage them to continue deep breathing while you teach.

Instruction

Today we will focus on a basic roadmap for regulation. In order to function at your best and use all levels of your brain, you need to be aware of the interventions that regulate each level.

Dr. Perry uses the terms **Regulate, Relate, Reason** to help you remember the importance of approaching regulation from the bottom of the brain up. He calls this the sequence of engagement. When the bottom regions of your brain are regulated, you are better able to relate to others. And when your relationships are safe and supportive, you can better access your cortex for learning, reasoning, and problem solving.[60]

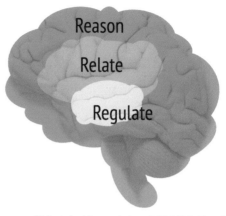

(Adapted with permission, © 2012 B.D. Perry)

Regulate, Relate, Reason is a mantra that has great practical applications. It can be a helpful reminder for yourself to practice ongoing interventions throughout the day, and to maintain regulation starting with the bottom of your brain and working your way up. It can also be very helpful when dealing with others who are dysregulated. It gives you a roadmap or sequence of steps to follow. Too often we try to reason with people who are upset and don't have access to their cortex. When you follow the wrong sequence of engagement, not only will you not be helpful, you will very likely make the situation worse. When pushed at the wrong level in this sequence, people will often feel even more threatened or unsafe and will say and do things that they will later regret.

You may have experienced an opportunity to use this sequence when finding yourself in an argument with a parent, friend, or loved one. When an argument gets heated, both people usually feel threatened and can move into a state of alarm of fear. As the lower areas of their brain take control, both people lose IQ points and move to reacting rather than relating. At this point, the words said become less and less helpful and more and more destructive. In a situation like this, if you can take a break from the argument before your lower brain regions take over and do something to help the lower levels of your brain stay regulated, you will be in a much better state to communicate and possibly solve the problem without so many regrettable and hurtful things being said. In an argument, one or both people often feel like they need to get in the last word and get angry if the other tries to walk away. Now that you recognize changing states of arousal, you may be able to stop the negative progression, give yourself and the other person permission to take a break, and allow time and space for each of you to calm down. This is very helpful when you find yourself angry and wanting to respond right away. Taking time to follow the sequence of engagement before responding is a wise approach to follow.

REGULATE

"Regulate" is the first part of this sequence of engagement. It refers to the physical calming strategies needed for the brainstem and midbrain. It is important to always start from the bottom of the brain and work your way up. When someone is in the fear or terror state, which may look like anger or rage, their brainstem or midbrain is in control. They are not thinking and are not focused on your relationship. They are reflexively acting or reacting to maintain their sense of safety.

The best thing you can do for someone in these states is to stay calm, give them space, keep them safe, and if you are aware of what works for them, give them what they need to calm down. A drink of water might be helpful for some as the act of drinking water requires a person to control and slow down their breathing. For others, allowing them to pace or walk might be helpful. Others might prefer wrapping themselves in a blanket or pulling a hoodie over their head. Some just need to get away and get involved in a physical task until they calm down. All the interventions you learned for the brainstem and midbrain, including the somatosensory and movement interventions, are helpful for regulating these bottom levels of the brain.

It is important to learn and practice calming skills ahead of time so you know what works for you when needed and you have developed some positive calming habits. If you work on regulation of the lower levels of your brain consistently, it can help you keep yourself in a calmer state for longer periods of time when faced with stress.

CALMING SKILLS ACTIVITY/DISCUSSION

Together with students make a list of things that work for regulating the brainstem and midbrain. Afterwards, use these prompts to encourage application and discussion:

- What from this list have you found that works for you? Write these things next to the "regulate" area in your workbook.
- List two new things you are willing to try in the upcoming weeks.
- Share with a classmate or in small groups at least one school-appropriate thing you have found that calms you. Is there a physical activity that helps calm you down (e.g. stretching, walking, yoga, weight lifting, or getting a drink of water)? What breathing or mindfulness skill that we have been learning do you think has the best chance of working for you? Have you been practicing or using this skill outside of class? If so, how is it going? If not, can you commit to practicing one this week?

Encourage students to also share what works for them and what triggers them with those who care about them. If you are triggered and move to a state controlled by the lower regions of your brain, you will not be able to access your cortex to choose the interventions needed at that time. Your brain will be reacting rather than choosing a response. When the people

"Once you understand how your body and brain are primed to react in certain situations, you can start to be proactive about how you approach things. You can identify triggers and know how to support yourself and those you love."[61]

NADINE BURKE HARRIS

who care about you understand this sequence of engagement, and know your triggers, they will be better prepared to help you get what you need to calm down and feel safe. They will also be less likely to respond in a way that makes things worse for you.

TRIGGERS ACTIVITY/DISCUSSION

Have students list some warning signs or triggers that could move someone into a state of alarm or fear when the situation is not necessarily physically dangerous. Have students write an individual list first and then share a few things from their list with the class as a whole. Make a combined list on the board. Encourage students to use ideas from the large list to make a personal list for themselves of warning signs or triggers. Use the following prompts for the students:
* Things that can trigger me to move to a state of alarm or fear are:
* If I am in a state of fear or alarm, the physical sensations that I may feel are:

It may be helpful to develop a written safety plan ahead of time, when you are calm and able to think clearly. Carry this with you and share a copy with those responsible for you. This may serve as a helpful reminder when you begin to feel stressed or unsafe as to what you can do about it. When you are triggered quickly into a lower region of your brain and not able to act on your safety plan, others who you have shared it with will be better prepared to help you feel and stay safe.

SAFETY PLAN ACTIVITY

Similar to what was done in Chapter 1, have students fill out a safety plan for bottom-up regulation. If they are comfortable and supportive of each other, they can work in pairs. If not, have them work individually. Allow students to share their plans if they want to.

RELATE

The second part of the sequence of engagement is "relate." This part is focused on the limbic system. Once you see that a person is regulated in the lower regions of their brain, you can focus on relationships and let them know they are safe and cared for. When the lower regions of their brains were in control, they were not able to take in this information.

Some of the signs that a person has become regulated in the lower regions of their brain might be:
* Their breathing slows down (or picks up if they were dissociating).
* Their muscle tension decreases.
* They are speaking in a more normal tone of voice.
* They are able to focus on what is happening around them and are no longer hyper focused on the perceived threat.
* They can look you in the eye and respond to what you are saying.

When functioning from the limbic system, people are still in a highly emotional and reactive state. Their thinking is not concrete and they are still not ready or able to make difficult decisions or solve problems. But in this state, they can and will respond to the calm, caring voice of someone with whom they feel safe. This is a good time to remind the person of the positive aspects of your relationship with him or her. You care for them, you will keep them safe, you are looking out for their best interest. Your words are not as important, at this point, as your nonverbal communication. They are very tuned into your emotions and your nonverbal expressions. Are you angry with them? Are you laughing at them? Did you just roll your eyes? Are you safe to be with? They need to feel your calmness and sense that you are in control. They need to feel loved and cared for. As their sense of safety grows and they are relationally regulated, their brain will allow them to move back into an alert state where the cortex is in control.

Not only is this relational regulation important when you are with someone you are trying to help regulate, it is an important aspect of your own regulation. When you are beginning to feel unsafe, struggling with relationships, and/or sensing your negative emotions rising in intensity, it is helpful to have built positive relationships with people who are able to stay calm, talk with you, help you, and possibly direct you to the strategies you need to regulate, relate, and regain your ability to reason.

It may be helpful to list the people in your life who are able to care for you in this way. Who are those closest to you who are able to calm you down when you are upset? Who do you have in school that is able to help you in this way? Is there anyone who you think might be able to fit into this category if you shared this information with them? If so, who? Are you willing to talk with them about this?

REASON

Once relational regulation has occurred, you can move to the "reason" part of the sequence. Only when a person is in a state of alert or calm are they able to reason, solve problems, and make thoughtful decisions. This last step in the sequence of engagement is where you are able to discuss the decisions that need to be made and what may happen next. Depending on how upset the person is, you will most likely need to give them more time before they can complete any heavy decision making, problem solving, or processing of what happened. The chemicals of stress stay in our bodies for hours, and pushing someone or yourself too hard at this point can easily retrigger a threat response.

It is helpful to make a list of all the interventions you have learned that work for you for each level of the brain in a regulate, relate, reason format. You may not always have access to all these interventions depending on what region of your brain is in control; however, having them thought through and written out in this regulate, relate, reason format will be helpful to remind you of the options available for regulation. When you are in a calm or alert state, you can use this as a checklist starting with the bottom regions of your brain and working your way up, making sure each region is regulated. Paying attention to this sequence will help you stay in as calm a state as possible throughout your day.

> "In between every action and reaction, there is a space. Usually the space is extremely small because we react so quickly, but take notice of that space and expand it. Be aware in that space that you have a choice to make."[62]
>
> **REBECCA EANES**

Reflection

This mindfulness exercise helps students be mindful of the tension in their bodies and works to bring about relaxation and calm.

PROGRESSIVE MUSCLE RELAXATION

In this exercise you apply muscle tension to a specific part of the body and then relax that muscle group. First, focus on the target muscle group, for example, your right hand. Next, take a slow, deep breath and squeeze the target muscle as hard as you can for about five seconds. It's important to feel the tension but not to hurt yourself. It is easy to accidentally tense other surrounding muscles but isolating muscle groups will get easier with practice. After five seconds, let the tightness flow out of tensed muscles. Exhale as you do this step. Allow the muscles to become loose and limp as tension flows out. Deliberately focus on the difference between the tension and relaxation. Remain in this relaxed state for about fifteen seconds and then move on to the next muscle group.

Walk the students through this exercise. To make it easier to remember, start with the feet and systematically move up to the forehead. After completing all the muscle groups let the students take some time to enjoy the deep state of relaxation.

Examples of muscle groups to target:

- Foot
- Lower leg and foot
- Entire leg
- Hand
- Arm
- Stomach
- Chest
- Neck and shoulders
- Mouth
- Eyes
- Forehead

Journal

Make sure each student has a journal and have art supplies available. Let students know journaling is their time to reflect and apply information learned in whatever way works for them. They can use words, colors, drawing or doodling.

Trauma, Neglect and Healing

Trauma, Neglect and Healing

Objectives & Materials

STUDENTS WILL BE ABLE TO:
- Define trauma
- Discuss the impact of trauma and neglect on the brain
- Recognize that trauma can affect people differently
- Define imprinting
- Identify steps to take in recovery from trauma

MATERIALS:
- Play dough
- Beads
- Stamp pads
- Ink

Making Connections

PLAY DOUGH ACTIVITY

Adapted from the work of Diane Wagenhals[63]

Have students each pick out a small tub of play dough and ask them to flatten it out. The flattened play dough represents their brain when they were younger. Have each student select a stamp that might represent some kind of vague memory (fun, somewhat scary, or emotional). Students should press the stamp or "memory" into their play dough or "brain." Have the students then roll their "brain" back into a ball. The stamp or "memory" disappears, similar to a memory that exists but is so deeply encoded that we don't think of it very often and have to be very intentional to remember it.

Have students flatten out their play dough again. Allow each student to pick a different stamp that could represent a fairly strong memory. This time use an inkpad and have students "imprint" the flattened play dough with the stamp and ink. Ask students to discuss the difference of having an "inked" imprint rather than just the stamp alone. (Possible responses: It will remain longer. It may get distorted as the brain grows and changes but, the ink still is part of the brain.)

Have students place pebbles or beads onto the stamped image. This represents events that are extremely sharp and wounding. After pushing the pebbles/beads into the play dough, students can roll it back into a ball.

Have students observe that although the pebbles/beads may no longer be visible, they can still be felt. They represent memories that have a lasting, embedded impact on the brain. Have students speculate on how this demonstration relates to trauma. (Possible response: Shows how powerful memories can be like shards of glass or rock distributed in different parts of the brain.) Explain that what is impacting one person in one area might not be impacting another person in that same area.

DISCUSSION:
* What is the difference in impact on the play dough between the ink and the pebbles?
* How do you think this might relate to the impact of trauma?

Preparing the Brain

Allow the students to choose a calming brain break from the list of those you have done so far, or have a student take the lead in sharing a brain break that they have found helpful.

Instruction

Before beginning to read the following article called "The Chowchilla Event," instructors should recognize that the intensity of this account may trigger some students. Let students know that sometimes when we read or hear about trauma and these terrible situations, they can bring up our own feelings of what has happened to us in the past. Recognize that this is okay and remind them of their safety plan for this classroom or group situation.

Either read, or have students take turns reading, the Chowchilla excerpt out loud. Interrupt at certain points as you deem appropriate to clarify what is happening, to answer questions, or to ask students to repeat details so you know they fully understand the article.

The following excerpt is a description of the Chowchilla Event written by Peter Levine in *Waking the Tiger: Healing Trauma*.[64]

On a sweltering day in 1976, twenty-six children ranging in age from five to fifteen years were kidnapped from their school bus outside a small California town. They were shoved into two dark vans, driven to an abandoned quarry, and then imprisoned in an underground vault for approximately thirty hours. They escaped, and were immediately taken to a local hospital. There, they received treatment for physical injuries, but were returned home without even cursory psychological examinations. As far as the two hospital physicians could tell, the children were "all right." The doctors simply did not recognize that anything was wrong or that the children's progress would need to be closely monitored. A few days later a local psychiatrist was asked to address the Chowchilla parents. He stated emphatically that there might be a psychological problem in only one of the twenty-six children. He was expressing the standard psychiatric belief at that time.

Eight months after the event, another psychiatrist, Lenore Terr, began one of the first scientific follow-up studies of children who had been traumatized. The study included these children. Rather than one in the twenty-six children showing aftereffects, Terr found the reverse to be true – nearly all of the children showed severe long-term effects on their psychological, medical and social functioning. For many of these children the nightmare had just begun. They experienced recurring nightmares, violent tendencies, and impaired ability to function normally in personal and social relations. The effects were so debilitating that the lives and family structures of these children were all but destroyed in the years that followed. The one child who was less severely affected was fourteen-year-old Bob Barklay. Here is a brief summary of what happened to him during the traumatic event.

The children had been imprisoned in "the hole" (a trailer buried beneath hundreds of pounds of dirt and rock in an abandoned quarry) for nearly a day when one of them leaned against a wooden pole that was supporting the roof. The makeshift support fell and the ceiling began to collapse on them. By this time, most of them were suffering from severe shock–frozen and apathetic they were almost unable to move. Those who realized the seriousness of the situation began to scream. These children could see that if they weren't able to escape soon, they would all die. It was in this moment of crisis that Bob Barklay enlisted the help of another boy to dig their way out. Following Bob's lead, the boys were able to scoop out enough dirt to dig a small tunnel through the ceiling and into the quarry. Bob was able to respond to the crisis and remain actively mobilized throughout the escape. Even though the other children escaped with him, many of them seemed to experience more fear in escaping their entombment. If they had not been urged strongly to flee, they would have remained there–helpless. Moving like zombies, they had to be ushered out to freedom. This passivity is similar to the behavior noted by military teams that specialize in the freeing of hostages. It is called the "Stockholm Syndrome". Often, hostages will not move unless repeatedly commanded to do so.

By bringing the other children to freedom, Bob Barklay successfully met an extraordinary challenge. On that day at Chowchilla, he was unquestionably a hero. However, what is more significant for his life, and for anyone interested in trauma, is that he emerged without the same degree of debilitating traumatic aftereffects as did the other twenty-five children. He was able to stay in motion and flow through the immobility response that completely overwhelmed and incapacitated the others. Some were so frightened that their fear continued to overwhelm and immobilize them long after the actual danger had passed.

DISCUSSION QUESTIONS

- What happened to the children in the story?
- How did medical emergency professionals initially respond to the children?
- In actuality, were the children okay?
- What does this account reveal to you about how trauma can impact people, even long after an event?

"Relational connectedness buffers current distress and helps heal past trauma."[66]

BRUCE D. PERRY

Although some professionals had already known the significant impact that trauma can have, in many ways the children that experienced this horrible event signified the beginning of our awareness of the impact of trauma on people and children specifically. The medical doctors in this situation thought there would be minimal long-term impact and the opposite was true for many of these children.

In our culture today, the word "trauma" is sometimes used informally to describe insignificant events. For example, someone may say that they were "traumatized" because they had their cell phone use limited, or because they had to wait in line for an hour at a store. In order to make sure we all have a foundational knowledge of what trauma is, here is a definition:

Not all fear-producing experiences create the same response in people. It is the response that determines whether the experience was traumatic, not the actual experience.

Wagenhals in Enhancing Trauma Awareness[67] tells us that while children are particularly vulnerable to being traumatized by the terrible things they experience, not all traumatic events will leave a lasting, traumatizing impact. There are several factors that can contribute to this. Every child is unique, and a combination of personality, temperament, observations, experiences, and support network contribute to how a child processes a traumatic event.

Another factor is how quickly comfort and safety are reestablished. The sooner there is intervention, the more likely that the event will have less long-standing traumatic results.

Therefore, some events that might be very traumatizing for one person may not be traumatizing at all for someone right next to them. For example, two people might be passengers in a car that was involved in a very serious accident. While both people might be very frightened at the time, one person may have a different perspective and some inner resiliency that allows him or her to recover emotionally within hours or days. Meanwhile, the other person might be so deeply affected as to become too frightened to ride in a car for weeks, months, or years.

DISCUSSION

Based on what you have learned so far, what suggestions would you have given to the doctors helping the children you read about today?

SENSORY MEMORIES

Trauma memories are stored as sensory memories. When someone is triggered and experiences a flashback, it most likely has its roots in the sensory memory areas of the lower brain.

We have spent much of our time learning about the remarkable nature of our brains, and how they develop and function as we grow. The brain stores memories, but not all of your experiences have an equal place in how they are stored. Like with the play dough, some memories are vague and it's hard to remember details unless you intentionally think very hard about them or are reminded by someone. Others become more strongly imprinted in your brain, and you can more easily recall details about the situation. Still other memories, particularly ones that are traumatic and painful, can be sharp and have an effect on the brain's development. Even after the situation or experience has ended, some memories can have a lasting impact on future situations we encounter. Some events are stored for a short time in our memory but other traumatic events are imprinted like beads, so that even when you can't see them, you still feel them and their impact.

THE IMPACT OF CHILDHOOD TRAUMA ON THE BRAIN

According to Dr. Perry, childhood trauma and neglect can have the following impacts:[68]

- A child can be traumatized through one overwhelmingly fear-producing event or many events over time.
- Trauma can occur when a child is attacked; physically, sexually or emotionally harmed; observes someone else being harmed; or believes he or she or a significant other is going to be harmed.
- Traumatized children have more trouble achieving a calm state, even at rest.
- When a trauma-based memory is triggered (by smells, sounds, shapes, visual cues, touches, words, or gestures) or a child feels at all threatened, he or she can instantaneously revert to a state of alarm or fear.
- When trauma occurs to girls or very young children, the result is often dissociation.
  - Dissociation can be described as "checking out," becoming disengaged, shutting down, distancing, and often having a lower heart rate.
- When trauma occurs to boys or older children, the result is usually hyper-arousal.
  - Hyper-arousal can be described as being and feeling on edge, acting in ways that are hyper-vigilant, "over-reactive," volatile, aggressive, and often having a higher heart rate.

"Trauma really does confront you with the best and the worst. You see the horrendous things that people do to each other, but you also see resiliency, the power of love, the power of caring, the power of commitment, the power of commitment to oneself, the knowledge that there are things that are larger than our individual survival."[69]

BESSEL VAN DER KOLK

STEPS TO RECOVERY FOR SOMEONE WHO HAS EXPERIENCED TRAUMA:[70]

- Make sure that you are safe. Recovery cannot start if the trauma is still ongoing in your life. If you are not safe, share this information with a trusted adult in your life.
- Many times, trauma can shatter self-esteem and self-worth. It is important to allow yourself to mourn over what is lost.
- Believe that you are capable and lovable to others.
- Reestablish relationships with people who will have a positive impact on your life—relationships that promote safety, creativity, and joy.
- Seek professional counseling. Trauma doesn't go away on its own. Talking about it with a professional can be a big help.

Reflection

Have students do a calming brain break or mindfulness activity. Choose one that you have seen work well in the past, or allow the students to choose.

Journal

Make sure each student has a journal and have art supplies available. Let students know journaling is their time to reflect and apply information learned in whatever way works for them. They can use words, colors, drawing or doodling.

CHAPTER 18

Next Steps

Next Steps

Objectives & Materials

STUDENTS WILL BE ABLE TO:
- Review what they have learned and record growth in a post-course survey
- Recognize protective factors that reduce the impact of trauma
- Design a personal plan for self-regulation
- Identify steps to take towards continued growth and/or recovery from trauma

MATERIALS:
- Quotations about trauma
- List of regulation activities
- Regulate, relate, reason worksheet
- Antwone Fisher DVD

Making Connections

Discuss what students are currently thinking about trauma and its impact. Share quotations from several professionals about healing from trauma. Hang them around the room. Have students read each quotation then stand by the one they like best. Have each student explain why they chose that quotation and what it means to them.

Here are some quotations that have been used throughout this course:

"Reflect upon your present blessings, of which every man has plenty; not on your past misfortunes, of which all men have some."
Charles Dickens

"Trauma really does confront you with the best and the worst. You see the horrendous things that people do to each other, but you also see resiliency, the power of love, the power of caring, the power of commitment, the power of commitment to oneself, the knowledge that there are things that are larger than our individual survival."
Bessel Van der Kolk

"Fire can warm or consume, water can quench or drown, wind can caress or cut. And so it is with human relationships: we can both create and destroy, nurture and terrorize, traumatize and heal each other."
Bruce D. Perry

"Psychologists say that having a grandparent who loves you, a teacher who understands and believes in you, or a trusted friend you can confide in may mitigate the long-term effects of early trauma."
Danny De Belius

"There are people with high ACE scores who do remarkably well. Resilience builds throughout life and close relationships are key."
Jack Shonkoff.

"The passion for stretching yourself and sticking to it, even (or especially) when it's not going well, is the hallmark of the growth mindset. This is the mindset that allows people to thrive during some of the most challenging times in their lives."
Carol S. Dweck

"For thirty years, my research has shown that the view you adopt for yourself profoundly affects the way you lead your life. It can determine whether you become the person you want to be and whether you accomplish the things you value."
Carol S. Dweck

"Failure is a part of life. It's a part of building character and growing. Without failure, who would you be? I wouldn't be here if I hadn't fallen thousands of times, made mistakes. . . . If something's going on in your life and you're struggling, embrace it, because you're growing."
Nick Foles, Super Bowl LII MVP

"Once you understand how your body and brain are primed to react in certain situations, you can start to be proactive about how you approach things. You can identify triggers and know how to support yourself and those you love."
Nadine Burke Harris

"Relational connectedness buffers current distress and helps heal past trauma." Bruce D. Perry

Preparing the Brain

GOTCHYA ACTIVITY
Adapted from *Energizing Brain Breaks*[71]

Do a fun brain break in partners that will get students laughing. Gotchya is a brain break developed by David Sladkey. In Gotchya, students stand in a circle or in small groups or partners, close enough to reach the person next to them. Each person puts their left hand out palm up and with their right hand they put their thumb down touching the palm of their partner or the person to their right. Everyone will have one hand out with a thumb touching it and one thumb out touching a hand. When the leader says, "gotchya," each person tries to simultaneously grab the thumb touching their left hand while keeping their thumb from being grabbed by their partner or the person on their right. You can repeat this several times. If you want to add variety, have them switch hands putting the opposite thumb down and palm out, or have them cross their arms across their chest and then do it.

Instruction

INTRODUCTION

As we have seen, the impact that trauma can have on brain development can be very powerful and detrimental. Talking about trauma can bring up some strong feelings, particularly if you have experienced trauma to some degree in your own life. The good news is that much can be done to help the brain recover and heal. This restoration, which means that the brain is rewired to a better condition, is possible. We've equipped you with many skills throughout this course to help develop and strengthen your brain. Today we will be reviewing all you have learned.

TOPICS COVERED:
- Creating safety plans
- The impact of perspective
- Brain plasticity
- The impact adverse experiences can have on your brain
- The capacity to counteract the impact of adverse experiences by developing each region of your brain
- Recognizing the roles of each brain region and what helps regulate them
- Your brain's natural responses to threat
- The impact of state-dependent functioning
- Using your senses and movement to regulate the lower regions of your brain
- The importance of relationships and impact of mirror neurons
- The connection of sensations and emotions
- The power of your thoughts and reasoning for regulation
- The sequence of engagement: regulate, relate, reason
- Trauma, neglect, and healing

Breathing exercises, mindfulness exercises, and all the other interventions we have explored are important as you continue to increase your self-regulation, which will in turn improve your relationships, your physical health, and your ability to reason.

ACTIVITIES

Give the students a list of all the activities you have done. As they look through this list, remind them that the activities target various parts of the brain and can help increase focus and concentration. Ask them to think

152

about the interventions you have done together and highlight which ones have worked well in helping them experience a greater sense of calm, a lower heart rate, and greater self-regulation.

- What have you experienced or learned that will help you better self-regulate?
- How can the information you have learned increase your self-control?

Have students check and update a final version of the regulate, relate, reason worksheet, and also review their safety plan for use when they find themselves operating from a lower region of the brain.

RIPPLE EFFECT

Show the last two scenes from *Antwone Fisher*. By the conclusion of the movie, Antwone grew emotionally, developed healthy relationships with a girlfriend and therapist, and began positively impacting others. Good relationships have a ripple effect.

Initially, Antwone was angry with his situation and was closed off to receiving any kind of help. With the persistence of his counselor, Antwone began the difficult journey to confront the trauma of his past. With much pain and hard work, Antwone confronted the hard memories and worked through the loss of broken relationships. Along the way, and unknown to Antwone, he began to also have a positive impact on those around him.

In our own journeys towards healing and making positive decisions that will give us a more hopeful future, we can have this same ripple effect on others. Just like Antwone's healing had a positive ripple effect on his counselor, his counselor's family, and then other patients, we too can have a ripple effect on others through our positive steps towards growth and healthy relationships.

Having been through this class, you've been empowered to take control of your own life. You can continue to learn and work on any areas of brain change and growth that you want. You can also have a positive impact on your relationships as you share this knowledge with others, and you will have a positive ripple effect, just like Antwone.

POST-COURSE SURVEY

Have students take the post-course survey. Afterwards, have them look back at their pre-course survey to see if their learning impacted their answers.

RIPPLE EFFECT ACTIVITY

Stand in a circle and have students hold hands or touch shoulders. One person begins and lightly squeezes the hand or shoulder of the person next to them. That person then squeezes the hand or shoulder of the person next to them. This continues on until the squeeze has gotten around the circle. You can then switch directions and send the squeeze back the other way. See how fast you can get it to go. Try keeping time of how long it takes to get around the circle and then see if you can beat your own record. You can also do this with a shake, a wobble, or any other movement of the hand.

Reflection

YOUR RIPPLE EFFECT

Present this closing reflection exercise:

Think about it. You are the center—as you make positive choices to change the course of your life, others will be impacted by your choices. Imagine yourself having made the changes you would like to make. You could think in terms of this month, year, or multiple years. Picture what it looks like. You are doing well. You are successful. Where are you, and what are you doing? Who is around you and how has your ripple effect impacted them? Continue to imagine having made the change or changes you want to make. Add as much detail to this picture as possible. Once you have a clear picture, draw or write about what you saw.

Journal

Make sure each student has a journal and have art supplies available. Let students know journaling is their time to reflect and apply information learned in whatever way works for them. They can use words, colors, drawing or doodling.

■ APPENDIX A

Additional Ideas

PIPE CLEANER ANALOGY

This analogy was developed by Kathryn J. deVries and is used with permission. If you choose to use this analogy, you can repeat it throughout the lessons, exemplifying how new connections are being made.

Our brain develops even before we are born. Basically, our brain functions by using a lot of neurons (which look like branches of a tree and can be represented by pipe cleaners). Each branch, or neuron, can release chemicals called neurotransmitters, which transmit a liquid form of communication back and forth between the neurons. Many of our neurons are formed when we are born, but each new experience creates a new branch of neurons in our brain. These little branches, or pathways, allow our thoughts to zip from one part of our brain to another.

Give each student a pile of six to ten colorful pipe cleaners in different sizes. Have them each make a shape like a tree. Discuss an experience the group has all had, such as eating a piece of fruit or a bowl of cereal. Ask them to talk about what neural connections in their brain might be represented by that experience. Show the first tree and talk about the apple itself. They might say it's round, red, and a bit soft. Each time they mention an adjective, you can point to a different color branch of the little tree. Hold up another little tree beside the first one and show how different areas of our brain can use the neurotransmitters to talk to other areas of the brain through these connections. (Put the tree branches near each other to demonstrate how the neurotransmitters release and go to the other tree.) Apple neural connections (first tree) might be connected or associated with neural connections for taste (hold up second tree) like sweet, tart, and cold.

Now pick an experience they are unlikely to have had, such as meeting the President of the United States. Hold up another tree. This is a neural network about the White House. Tie a new color pipe cleaner to your tree and explain how a new experience such as meeting the President would create new neural connections in the brain. Now when they think of the White House, they have this branch that leads to a memory of meeting the President.

We can intentionally create new neural networks! It might feel a little scary because our brain pays close attention to information that doesn't fit anywhere in our neural networks. Our brain needs to decide if that information tells us we are in danger. If you decide to learn to play basketball at a new place like the YMCA, your brain is going to start to send signals to make sure this experience is safe. If you push yourself through the brain's warnings, you will build some new neural networks like basketball connected to laughter, strength, and fun.

If you are a counselor, you may choose to go in a trauma direction. You could pick an experience that the students are unlikely to have had, such as being chased by a lion or being in a giant storm out at sea. They would not have any neural connections (pipe cleaner branches) for that experience. That is what trauma is like. A neural connection is formed quickly (make a messy tree). We don't have other experiences to connect it to because it is so overwhelming and unorganized. Hold the messy tree away from the others and demonstrate how that experience is isolated. What we do in counseling is try to find experiences and ideas that students can use to integrate or connect that trauma experience to what they already know about the world. This helps us break it down and make it easier to respond to it. Hold up the messy tree and start attaching new pieces and straightening it. Throw out healthy things they might attach to the trauma experience. Examples might be: "We might find areas of strength and skill we used during that trauma." "We kept ourselves alive through it." "We handled it without a safe adult."

As we examine our negative experiences in trauma situations, we consider what experiences this blocked us from having, such as close friendships or a feeling of safety. These are neural connections we want to experience. It might feel a little scary because our brain pays close attention to information that doesn't fit anywhere in our neural networks. Our brain needs to decide if that information tells us we are in danger. If we weren't safe, our brain might keep warning us a new friend might hurt us like in a previous experience. We may have to move slowly to get to know that person. Adding new experiences and neural pathways at a pace that feels safe for our brain will help us build a solid neural network for how to be friends.

HAND AS BRAIN MODEL ANALOGY

Dan Siegel uses a hand as a model for the brain. https://www.youtube.com/watch?v=gm9CIJ74Oxw

This is a helpful analogy and easy for students to remember. Hold your arm up with your hand in a fist. The bottom of your palm connected to your wrist represents the brainstem. When you raise your fingers straight up, you can see the palm and thumb which represents the midbrain and limbic system. The fingers folded down over the thumb represent the cortex. When you raise the fingers, you exemplify what happens when the brain senses danger. The cortex goes offline and is temporarily not available for decision making. Or, as Dan Siegel puts it, we "flip our lid."

Notes

INTRODUCTION

1   Zull, J. (2002). *The Art of Changing the Brain*. Sterling, VA: Stylus Publishing, pp. 91-110, copyright © by Stylus Publishing, LLC.

2   Medina, J. (2008). *Brain Rules*. Seattle, WA: Pear Press, p. 240, copyright © 2014 by John J. Medina.

3   Wagenhals, L.D. (2018). Ideas for brain region visuals have come from the training of Diane Wagenhals and used with permission, copyright ©2018 by L. Diane Wagenhals and Lakeside.

4   MacNeill, J. (2017). *101 Brain Breaks & Brain Based Educational Activities*. North Wales, PA: Lakeside. Used with permission, copyright ©2017 by Lakeside Youth Service.

5   Meiklejohn, J., Phillips, C., Freedman, M.L. et al. *Mindfulness* (2012). 3: 291. https://doi.org/10.1007/s12671-012-0094-5, copyright © 2012 by Springer Science+Business Media, LLC.

CHAPTER 1: CREATING SAFETY

6   Bloom, S. L. (1997 and 2013). *Creating Sanctuary: Toward the Evolution of Sane Societies*. New York, NY: Routledge, copyright © 1997 by Routledge.

7   Wagenhals, L. D. and Lakeside. (2018). *Enhancing Trauma Awareness Training*. North Wales, PA: Lakeside, copyright © 2018 by L. Diane Wagenhals and Lakeside.

8   Biegel, G. M. (2016, June 20). *Mindfulness-Based Stress Reduction*. PESI seminar presented at King of Prussia, PA.

CHAPTER 2: IMPACT OF PERSPECTIVE

9   Brain Facts for Kids. (2016). Retrieved from http://www.coolkidfacts.com/facts-about-the-brain-for-kids/ Copyright © 2016 by CoolKidFacts.

10 Adapted from Hiebert, M., Platt, J., Schpok, K.& Whitesel, J. (2013). *Doodles, Dances and Ditties: A Trauma-Informed Somatosensory Handbook*. Denver, CO: Mount Saint Vincent Home, copyright © 2013 by Mount Saint Vincent Home.

11 Browning E. B. (n. d.). *AZQuotes.com*. Retrieved from http://www.azquotes.com/quote/673994

12 Foles, N. (2018, February 5). *Nick Foles Amazing Super Bowl Postgame Speech* (Video file). Retrieved from https://www.youtube.com/watch?v=0vrlW3YP_Bg

13 Dweck, C. (2016). *Mindset: The New Psychology of Success*. New York: NY: Random House, p. 6, copyright © 2006, 2016 by Carol S. Dweck, Ph.D.

14 Dweck, C. (2016). *Mindset: The New Psychology of Success*. New York: NY: Random House.

15 Dweck, C. (2016). *Mindset: The New Psychology of Success*. New York: NY: Random House, pp. 228-231.

16 Dweck, C. (2016). *Mindset, The New Psychology of Success*. New York, NY: Random House, p. 7.

CHAPTER 3: UNDERSTANDING BRAIN PLASTICITY

17 Altman, D. (2014). *The Mindfulness Toolbox*. Eau Claire, WI: Pesi Publishing and Media, pp. 29-33. Used with permission, copyright © 2013 by Donald Altman, M.A., LPC.

18 Adapted from Handwerk, B. (2004, May 14). *Sea Gypsies of Asia Boast "Incredible" Underwater Vision*. National Geographic Ultimate Explorer. Retrieved from https://news.nationalgeographic.com/news/2004/05/0514_040514_seagypsies.html

19 Handwerk, B. (2004, May 14). *Sea Gypsies of Asia Boast "Incredible" Underwater Vision*.

National Geographic Ultimate Explorer. Retrieved from https://news.nationalgeographic.com/news/2004/05/0514_040514_seagypsies.html

20 *How Moken children see with amazing clarity underwater* (Video file). (2011, May 16). Retrieved from https://www.youtube.com/watch?v=YIKm3Pq9U8M

21 Information on brain plasticity through various stages is based on a compilation of the work and research of Bruce D. Perry and the ChildTrauma Academy. This includes the Articles, DVDs and YouTube videos listed in the resource section, Appendix C. A specific resource is Perry, B. D. (2013, September 6). The ChildTrauma Academy Channel. *SevenSlideSeries: The Human Brain* (Video file). Retrieved from https://www.youtube.com/watch?v=uOsgDkeH52o

22 Steinberg, L. (2014). *Age of Opportunity: Lessons from the New Science of Adolescence.* New York, New York: First Mariner Books, p.24. copyright © 2014 by Lawrence Steinberg.

23 Perry, B. D. (1999). *Memories of Fear: How the Brain Stores and Retrieves Physiologic States, Feelings, Behaviors and Thoughts from Traumatic Events.* ChildTrauma Academy version. Retrieved from https://childtrauma.org/wpcontent/uploads/2014/12/Memories_of_Fear_Perry.pdf

24 Sandlin, D. (2015, April 24). *The Backwards Brain Bicycle-Smarter Every Day* (Video File). Retrieved from https://www.youtube.com/user/destinws2

25 Adapted from Zadina, J. N. (2014). *Multiple Pathways to the Student Brain: Energizing and Enhancing Instruction.* San Francisco, CA: Jossey-Bass, p. 13, copyright ©2014 by John Wiley & Sons, Inc.

26 Street Wisdom Billy. (2011, July 3). *Brain Plasticity the Story of Jody* (Video file). Retrieved from https://www.youtube.com/watch?v=VaDlLD97CLM

27 Young, B. A. (2016, October 27). *The Women Who Changed Her Brain: Barbara Arrowsmith Young at Tedx Toronto* (Video file). Retrieved from https://www.youtube.com/watch?v=oKds1vlxOVA

28 Doidge, N. (2007). *The Brain That Changes Itself: Stories of Personal Triumph from the Frontiers of Brain Science.* New York, NY: Penguin Books, pp. 20-23, copyright © 2007 by Norman Doidge.

CHAPTER 4: ADVERSE CHILDHOOD EXPERIENCES

29 Wagenhals, L. D. and Lakeside. (2018). *Enhancing Trauma Awareness Training.* North Wales, PA: Lakeside.

30 Adapted from Hiebert, M., Platt, J., Schpok, K.& Whitesel, J. (2013). *Doodles, Dances and Ditties: A Trauma-Informed Somatosensory Handbook.* Denver, CO: Mount Saint Vincent Home.

31 Felitti, V. J., Anda, R. F., Nordenberg, D., Williamson, D. F., Spitz, A. M., Edwards, V., ... Marks, J. S. (1998). "Relationship of childhood abuse and household dysfunction to many of the leading causes of death in adults: The adverse childhood experiences (ACE) study". *American Journal of Preventive Medicine, 14*(4), 245-258. DOI: 10.1016/S0749-3797(98)00017-8, copyright © 1998 by American Journal of Preventive Medicine.

32 Anda, R. (n. d.). *Letter from Dr. Anda: Community Resilience Cookbook.* Retrieved from http://communityresiliencecookbook.org/robert-anda-intro/, copyright © 2018 by Community Resilience Cookbook.

33 Starecheski, L. (2015, March 2). *Take the ACE Quiz- And Learn What It Does and Doesn't Mean.* Retrieved from https://www.npr.org/sections/health-shots/2015/03/02/387007941/take-the-ace-quiz-and-learn-what-it-does-and-doesnt-mean

34 Perry, B. D. (2009). "Examining Child Maltreatment Through a Neurodevelopmental Lens: Clinical Applications of the Neurosequential Model of Therapeutics". Journal of Loss and Trauma, 14:240-255, copyright © 2009 by Taylor & Francis Group, LLC and Perry, B. D. and Szalavitz, M. (2017). *The Boy Who Was Raised as a Dog: And Other Stories from a Child Psychiatrist's Notebook.* New York, NY: Basic Books, pp. 327-330, copyright ©2006, 2017 by Bruce Perry and Maria Szalavitz.

35 Debelius, D. (n. d.). *Adverse Experiences (ACES) Quiz.* Retrieved from https://www.safelaunch.org/aces-quiz/, copyright © 2018 by SafeLaunch.

CHAPTER 5: RECOGNIZING BRAIN REGIONS

36 Adapted from Hiebert, M., Platt, J., Schpok, K.& Whitesel, J. (2013). *Doodles, Dances and Ditties: A Trauma-Informed Somatosensory Handbook.* Denver, CO: Mount Saint Vincent Home.

37 This chapter as well as those that follow are adapted with permission from the Neurosequential Model of Therapeutics (NMT) and the Neurosequential Model of Education (NME) developed by the ChildTrauma Academy. The information here and in the chapters that follow is a compilation of things learned while completing the requirements for NMT and NME certification. Some helpful articles, DVDs and YouTube videos that were a part of this training are listed in the resource section, Appendix C.

CHAPTER 7: MIDBRAIN

38 Adapted from Dennison, P. E. and Dennison, G. E. (1994). *Brain Gym®: Teachers Edition, Revised. Ventura,* CA: Edu-Kinesthetics Inc., copyright ©1989, 1994 and 2010 by Paul E Dennison and Gail E. Dennison. Brain Gym® is a registered trademark of the Educational Kinesiology Foundation in Santa Barbara, CA. For more information about the Brain Gym program visit www.braingym.org

39 Andrade, J. (2010). "What does doodling do?". *Applied Cognitive Psychology,* 24(1), 100-106, copyright © 2009 by John Wiley & Sons Ltd.

CHAPTER 8: LIMBIC SYSTEM

40 Perry, B. D. (2014, January 14). *Six Core Strengths for Healthy Child Development: An Overview* (Video file). Retrieved from https://www.youtube.com/watch?v=skaYWKC6iD4 and Perry B. D. and Szalavitz, M. (2010). *Born for Love: Why Empathy is Essential – and Endangered.* New York, NY: HarperCollins Publishers, copyright © 2010 by Maria Szalavitz and Bruce D. Perry.

CHAPTER 9: CORTEX

41 Doidge, N. (2007). *The Brain That Changes Itself: Stories of Personal Triumph from the Frontiers of Brain Science.* New York, NY: Penguin Books, p.252.

42 Emmons, R. A. and McCullough, M. E. (2003). "Counting Blessings Versus Burdens: An Experiential Investigation of Gratitude and Subjective Well-Being in Daily Life". *Journal of Personality and Social Psychology.* Vol 84, No 2, 377-389, copyright © 2003 by the American Psychological Association, Inc.

CHAPTER 10: RESPONSES TO THREAT

43 Specific resources on this topic include The ChildTrauma Academy Channel. (2013, December 31). *SevenSlideSeries: The Threat Response Patterns* (Video file). Retrieved from https://www.youtube.com/watch?v=sr-OXkk3i8E and The ChildTrauma Academy Channel.

(2014, February 14). *SevenSlideSeries: State-Dependent Functioning* (Video file). Retrieved from https://www.youtube.com/watch?v=1uCn7VX6BPQ

APTER 11: STATE-DEPENDENT FUNCTIONING

44 Dennison, P. E. and Dennison, G. E. (1994). *Brain Gym®, Teachers Edition, Revised.* Ventura, CA: Edu-Kinesthetics Inc. Brain Gym® is a registered trademark of the Educational Kinesiology Foundation in Santa Barbara, CA. For more information about the Brain Gym program visit www.braingym.org

45 Specific resources on this topic include The ChildTrauma Academy Channel. (2014, February 14). *SevenSlideSeries: State-Dependent Functioning* (Video file). Retrieved from https://www.youtube.com/watch?v=1uCn7VX6BPQ and Perry, B. D. and Szalavitz, M. (2017). *The Boy Who Was Raised as a Dog: And Other Stories from a Child Psychiatrist's Notebook.* New York, NY: Basic Books, pp. 296-302.

46 Zidane head butt story. (2014, July 30). Retrieved from http://www.football-bible.com/soccer-info/zidane-head-butt-story.html

CHAPTER 12: SOMATOSENSORY REGULATION

47 MacNeill, J. (2017). *101 Brain Breaks & Brain Based Educational Activities.* North Wales, PA: Lakeside.

48 Perry, B. D. (2001, November). "Self-Regulation: The Second Core Strength". *Early Childhood Today, Volume 16, Issue 3,* p.20.

49 Cook, J. L. and Cook, G. (2009). *Child Development Principles and Perspectives, 2nd Edition.* New York, NY: Pearson, p. 36, copyright © 2009 by Pearson.

50 Williams, M. S. and Shellenberger, S. (2001). *Take Five! Staying Alert at Home and School.* Albuquerque, NM: Therapy Works Inc., copyright ©2001 by Therapy Works, Inc.

51 Aquilla, P., Yack, E. and Sutton, S. (2015). *Building Bridges Through Sensory Integration.* Arlington, TX: Sensory World, p. 45, copyright © 2015 by E. Yack, S. Sutton, P. Aquilla.

52 Aquilla, P., Yack, E. and Sutton, S. (2015). *Building Bridges Through Sensory Integration.* Arlington, TX: Sensory World, p. 48.

CHAPTER 13: EMOTIONS AND SENSATIONS

53 Wagenhals, L. D. and Lakeside. (2018). *Applying Trauma Principles Training.* North Wales, PA: Lakeside, copyright © 2018 by L. Diane Wagenhals and Lakeside.

54 Murray, C. (2018). *Emotion Works: An educational programme for the development of emotional language and understanding,* copyright © 2018 by Emotion Works CIC. Found at https://www.emotionworks.org.uk/

55 Goleman, D. (1995). *Emotional Intelligence: Why It Can Matter More Than IQ.* New York, NY: Bantam Books, copyright © 1995 by Daniel Goleman.

CHAPTER 14: RELATIONAL REGULATION

56 Silverstein, S. (1964). *The Giving Tree.* New York, NY: Harper & Row, Publishers, copyright © 1964 by Snake Eye Music, Inc.

57 Perry, B. D. and Szalavitz, M. (2017). *The Boy Who Was Raised as a Dog: And Other Stories from a Child Psychiatrist's Notebook.* New York, NY: Basic Books, p. xxviii, copyright © 2006, 2017 by Bruce Perry and Maria Szalavitz.

CHAPTER 15: CORTICAL REGULATION

58 MacNeill, J. (2017). *101 Brain Breaks & Brain Based Educational Activities*. North Wales, PA: Lakeside.

59 Woods, J. (1899). *Dictionary of Quotations*. London, NY: Frederick Warne & Co., Bartleby.com, 2012. Retrieved from www.bartleby.com/345/authors/140.html Copyright © 2012 by Bartleby.com

CHAPTER 16: REGULATE, RELATE, REASON

60 Perry, B. D. (2014). Neurosequential Inaugural Model Symposium. I first heard Dr. Perry speak about "Regulate, Relate, Reason" at the Symposium in Banff, Canada, June, 2014. Information can also be found in Perry, B. D. and Szalavitz, M. (2017). *The Boy Who Was Raised as a Dog: And Other Stories from a Child Psychiatrist's Notebook*. New York, NY: Basic Books, pp. 303-304.

61 Harris, N. B. (2018). The Deepest Well: Healing the Long-Term Effects of Childhood Adversity. New York, NY: Houghton Mifflin Harcourt, p. 218, copyright © 2018 by Nadine Burke Harris.

62 Eanes, R. (2015). *The Newbie's Guide to Positive Parenting: 2nd Edition*. N. Charleston, SC: CreateSpace Independent Publishing Platform, p. 40, copyright © by Rebecca Eanes.

CHAPTER 17: TRAUMA, NEGLECT AND HEALING

63 Wagenhals, L. D. and Lakeside. (2018). *Enhancing Capacity for Applying Trauma Principles Training*. North Wales, PA: Lakeside, copyright © 2018 by L. Diane Wagenhals and Lakeside.

64 Levine, P. with Frederick, A. (1997). *Waking the Tiger: Healing Trauma*. Berkeley, CA: North Atlantic Books, pp. 26-28, copyright © 1997 by Peter A. Levine. Reprinted by permission of publisher.

65 James, B. (1989). *Treating Traumatized Children: New Insights and Creative Interventions*. New York, NY: The Free Press, p. 1, copyright © 1989 by The Free Press.

66 Perry, B. D. and Szalavitz, M. (2017). *The Boy Who Was Raised as a Dog: And Other Stories from a Child Psychiatrist's Notebook*. New York, NY: Basic Books, p. 328.

67 Wagenhals, L. D. and Lakeside. (2018). *Enhancing Trauma Awareness Training*. North Wales, PA: Lakeside.

68 This is adapted from the training of the ChildTrauma Academy and many of the resources listed in appendix C. A specific resource is Perry, B. D. (2006). "Applying Principles of Neurodevelopment to Clinical Work with Maltreated and Traumatized Children", In Webb, N. B. (Ed.) *Working with Traumatized Youth in Child Welfare*. New York, NY: Guilford Press, pp. 27-52, copyright © 2006 by Guilford Press.

69 Van der Kolk, B. A. (2013, July 11). *Restoring the Body: Yoga, EMDR, and Treating Trauma*. OnBeing. (K. Tippett, Interviewer) (Audio file). Retrieved from https://onbeing.org/programs/bessel-van-der-kolk-restoring-body-yoga-emdr-treating-trauma/

70 Adapted from the work of Wagenhals, L. D. and Lakeside. (2018). *Enhancing Trauma Awareness Training*. North Wales, PA: Lakeside.

CHAPTER 18: NEXT STEPS

71 Sladkey, D. (2013). *Energizing Brain Breaks*. Thousand Oaks, CA: Corwin, copyright © 2013 by David Sladkey. Used with permission.

Resources and Worksheets

Altman, D. (2014). *The Mindfulness Toolbox.* Eau Claire, WI: Pesi Publishing and Media.

Antwone Fisher DVD. Copyright © 2011 by Twentieth Century Fox Home Entertainment, LLC.

Bloom, S. L. (1997 and 2013). *Creating Sanctuary: Toward the Evolution of Sane Societies.* New York, NY: Routledge.

Bloom, S. L. and Farragher, B. (2013). *Restoring Sanctuary: A New Operating System for Trauma-Informed Systems of Care.* New York, NY, Oxford University Press.

Chapin, B. (2014). *Helping Teens Learn Self-Regulation.* Chapin, SC: YouthLight Inc., copyright © 2016, 2014 YouthLight, Inc.

Dennison, P. E. and Dennison, G. E. (1994). *Brain Gym®, Teachers Edition, Revised.* Ventura, CA: Edu-Kinesthetics Inc.

Doidge, N. (2015). *The Brain's Way of Healing.* New York, NY: Viking.

Doidge, N. (2007). *The Brain That Changes Itself: Stories of Personal Triumph from the Frontiers of Brain Science.* New York, NY: Penguin Books.

Dweck, C. (2006). *Mindset: The New Psychology of Success.* New York, NY: Random House.

Harris, N. B. (2018). *The Deepest Well: Healing the Long-Term Effects of Childhood Adversity.* New York, NY: Houghton Mifflin Harcourt.

Harris, N. B. (2015, February 17). *How childhood trauma affects health across a lifetime.* Retrieved at https://www.youtube.com/watch?v=95ovIJ3dsNk

Lakeside Global Institute. (2018). Trauma Training available at www.lakesidelink.com/training

Levine, P. A. with Frederick, A. (1997). *Waking the Tiger: Healing Trauma.* Berkeley, CA: North Atlantic Books.

Levine, P. A. and Kline, M. (2007). *Trauma Through a Child's Eyes: Awakening the Ordinary Miracle of Healing.* Berkeley, CA: North Atlantic Books, copyright © 2007 by Peter A. Levine and Maggie Kline.

MacNeill, J. (2017). *101 Brain Breaks & Brain Based Educational Activities.* North Wales, PA: Lakeside.

Murray, C. (2018). *Emotion Works: An educational program for the development of emotional language and understanding.* Retrieved from https://www.emotionworks.org.uk/

Perry, B. D. and Szalavitz, M. (2017). *The Boy Who Was Raised as a Dog: And Other Stories from a Child Psychiatrist's Notebook.* New York, NY: Basic Books.

Perry B. D. and Szalavitz, M. (2010). *Born for Love: Why Empathy is Essential – and Endangered.* New York, NY: HarperCollins Publishers.

Perry, B. D., Pollard, R.A., Blakely, T.I. and Vigilante, D. (1995) "Childhood Trauma, the Neurobiology of Adaptation and 'Use Dependent' Development of the Brain, how 'States' become 'Traits' *Infant Medical Health Journal,* 16(4):271-29.

Perry, B. D. (1999). "*Memories of Fear: How the Brain Stores and Retrieves Physiologic States, Feelings, Behaviors and Thoughts from Traumatic Events*". CTA Academy version. Retrieved from https://childtrauma.org/wpcontent/uploads/2014/12/Memories_of_Fear_Perry.pdf

Perry, B. D. (2004). "Understanding Traumatized and Maltreated Children". The *ChildTrauma Academy and Linkletter Films.* DVD series, copyright © 2004 by Linkletter Media & ChildTrauma Academy.

Perry, B. D. (2006). "Applying Principles of Neurodevelopment to Clinical Work with Maltreated and Traumatized Children", In Webb, N. B. (Ed.) *Working with Traumatized Youth in Child Welfare.* New York, NY: Guilford Press, copyright © 2006 by Guilford Press.

Perry, B. D. (2008). "The Neurosequential Model of Therapeutics: Practical Applications for Traumatized and Maltreated Children at Home, in the School and in Clinical Settings". The *ChildTrauma Academy DVD series,* copyright © 2008 by The ChildTrauma Academy.

Perry, B. D. (2009). "Examining Child Maltreatment Through a Neurodevelopmental Lens: Clinical Applications of the Neurosequential Model of Therapeutics". *Journal of Loss and Trauma,* 14:240-255.

Perry, B. D. (2013, September 6). The ChildTrauma Academy Channel. *SevenSlideSeries: The Human Brain* (Video file). Retrieved from https://www.youtube.com/watch?v=uOsgDkeH52o

Perry, B. D. (2013, September 17). The ChildTrauma Academy Channel. *SevenSlideSeries: Sensitization and Tolerance* (Video file). Retrieved from https://www.youtube.com/watch?v=qv8dRfgZXV4

Perry, B. D. (2013, December 31). The ChildTrauma Academy Channel. *SevenSlideSeries: The Threat Response Patterns* (Video file). Retrieved from https://www.youtube.com/watch?v=sr-OXkk3i8E

Perry, B. D. (2014, January 14). *Six Core Strengths for Healthy Child Development: An Overview* (Video file). Retrieved from https://www.youtube.com/watch?v=skaYWKC6iD4

Perry, B. D. (2014, February 14). The ChildTrauma Academy Channel. *SevenSlideSeries: State-Dependent Functioning* (Video file). Retrieved from https://www.youtube.com/watch?v=1uCn7VX6BPQ

Williams, M. S. and Shellenberger, S. (2001). *Take Five! Staying Alert at Home and School*. Albuquerque, NM: Therapy Works Inc.

Sladkey, D. (2013). *Energizing Brain Breaks*. Thousand Oaks, CA: Corwin.

Thumb Balls can be purchased at www.thumball.com

Van de Kolk, B. A. (2014). *The Body Keeps Score: Brain, Mind and Body in the Healing of Trauma*. New York, NY: Penguin Books.

Zadina, J. N. (2014). *Multiple Pathways to the Student Brain: Energizing and Enhancing Instruction*. San Francisco, CA: Jossey-Bass.

Pre-Course Student Survey

Name _____ Date _____

Directions: Read the following statements and circle the answer that best describes you.

1. I believe my brain can change based on experiences and repeated practice.
    Strongly Disagree   Disagree   Unsure   Agree   Agree Strongly

2. I can name the four regions of the brain and tell you what they are responsible for.
    Strongly Disagree   Disagree   Unsure   Agree   Agree Strongly

3. I know several strategies to help me stay calm in stressful situations.
    Strongly Disagree   Disagree   Unsure   Agree   Agree Strongly

4. I recognize the physical sensations that let me know I am getting frustrated or angry.
    Strongly Disagree   Disagree   Unsure   Agree   Agree Strongly

5. I understand why I am not able to think clearly when I am anxious, angry or upset, and I know what to do to change this.
    Strongly Disagree   Disagree   Unsure   Agree   Agree Strongly

6. I can name the five continuum states ranging from calm to terror and recognize these states when I have experienced them.
    Strongly Disagree   Disagree   Unsure   Agree   Agree Strongly

7. I understand the impact of adverse experiences on the brain.
    Strongly Disagree   Disagree   Unsure   Agree   Agree Strongly

8. I have many things in my life to be thankful for.
    Strongly Disagree   Disagree   Unsure   Agree   Agree Strongly

9. I know and use breathing exercises to help me remain calm and alert.
    Strongly Disagree   Disagree   Unsure   Agree   Agree Strongly

10. I know how to use mindfulness exercises to help me in various situations.
    Strongly Disagree   Disagree   Unsure   Agree   Agree Strongly

Post-Course Student Survey

Name _____ Date _____

Directions: Read the following statements and circle the answer that best describes you.

1. I believe my brain can change based on experiences and repeated practice.
    Strongly Disagree   Disagree   Unsure   Agree   Agree Strongly

2. I can name the four regions of the brain and tell you what they are responsible for.
    Strongly Disagree   Disagree   Unsure   Agree   Agree Strongly

3. I know several strategies to help me stay calm in stressful situations.
    Strongly Disagree   Disagree   Unsure   Agree   Agree Strongly

4. I recognize the physical sensations that let me know I am getting frustrated or angry.
    Strongly Disagree   Disagree   Unsure   Agree   Agree Strongly

5. I understand why I am not able to think clearly when I am anxious, angry or upset, and I know what to do to change this.
    Strongly Disagree   Disagree   Unsure   Agree   Agree Strongly

6. I can name the five continuum states ranging from calm to terror and recognize these states when I have experienced them.
    Strongly Disagree   Disagree   Unsure   Agree   Agree Strongly

7. I understand the impact of adverse experiences on the brain.
    Strongly Disagree   Disagree   Unsure   Agree   Agree Strongly

8. I have many things in my life to be thankful for.
    Strongly Disagree   Disagree   Unsure   Agree   Agree Strongly

9. I know and use breathing exercises to help me remain calm and alert.
    Strongly Disagree   Disagree   Unsure   Agree   Agree Strongly

10. I know how to use mindfulness exercises to help me in various situations.
    Strongly Disagree   Disagree   Unsure   Agree   Agree Strongly

My Safety Plan

Name _____

Directions: List some things you can do to keep yourself feeling safe. Include both internal and external options.

While in class, I can do the following things to stay safe:

1. _____

2. _____

3. _____

4. _____

5. _____

6. _____

In other situations, I can do the following things to stay safe (list both the situation and the strategy):

1. _____

2. _____

3. _____

4. _____

5. _____

6. _____

Perspective Survey

Name _____

Circle the one statement in each pair that you believe best reflects the way you think.

1. If I am not good at something, I probably never will be.

2. If I stick with something, I can get better at it.

1. If my first plan fails, I give up.

2. If my first plan fails, I can figure out another way to do it.

1. Making mistakes is embarrassing.

2. Making mistakes is a chance to learn how to do it better next time.

1. My beliefs about people and the world are accurate and will not change.

2. My beliefs about people and the world are flexible and change with experiences.

1. You can only get straight As if you are naturally smart.

2. Anyone can get straight As if they work hard enough.

1. If you are impulsive, you will always be that way.

2. You can change how impulsive you are.

Count the number of 1s and 2s that you circled and record that below.

Number of 1s _____

Number of 2s _____

Brain Regions

Name _____

Write down what you learned about each region of the brain.

The Brainstem:

(Adapted with permission, © 2012 B.D. Perry)

The Midbrain:

(Adapted with permission, © 2012 B.D. Perry)

The Limbic System:

(Adapted with permission, © 2012 B.D. Perry)

The Cortex:

(Adapted with permission, © 2012 B.D. Perry)

State-Dependent Functioning

Name _____

Write down what you learned about each state.

Calm

Cortex •————————— Calm / Alert

Limbic •————————— Alarm

Midbrain •————————— Fear

Brainstem •————————— Terror

(Adapted with permission, © 2012 B.D. Perry)

Alert

Alarm

Fear

Terror

Understanding Your Sensory Preferences

Name _____

TASTE ▪ What are some things you eat, drink, or chew to calm down?

What are some things you eat, drink, or chew to wake up?

TOUCH ▪ What are some school-appropriate ways your sense of touch can calm you down?

What are some school-appropriate ways your sense of touch can wake you up?

SMELL ▪ Are there any smells you find calming?

Which smells energize you?

SOUND ▪ What music or sounds help to calm you down?

What music or sounds tend to energize you?

VISUAL ▪ Is there something visual that you can look at to calm yourself down?

Are there pictures, colors, or other visuals that energize you?

Emotions and Sensations

Name _____

List or draw the sensation you feel with each of the following emotions:

Happy
Sad

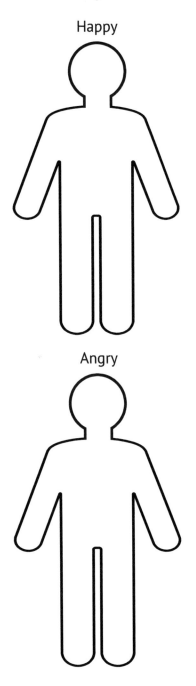

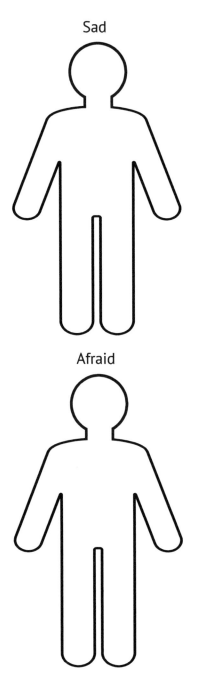

Angry
Afraid

Regulate, Relate, Reason

Name _____

List things you have learned that can help you calm down using each level of the brain. Remember the importance of focusing your efforts from the bottom up.

Reason

Relate

Regulate

(Adapted with permission, © 2012 B.D. Perry)

Physical Regulation

Relational Regulation

Regulation through Reasoning